THERE IS ... WHISTLEBLOWER EDITION TWO

Eileen Chubb

chipmunkapublishing
the mental health publisher

Published by
Chipmunkapublishing
United Kingdom

http://www.chipmunkapublishing.com

Copyright © 2020 Eileen Chubb

ISBN   978-1-78382-515-8

Dedication

For every person who has ever been harmed or died for the want of a Whistle-blower being heard.

For every Whistle-blower who has suffered injustice, for the want of the rule of law.
For all those who believed in Edna's Law from the start, especially Stephen Honour, whose support made this possible.

Thank you to Christine England for proof reading and for her friendship.

To everyone who signed the petition for Edna's Law and who have supported and stood with Edna. There are far too many people to name everyone and I fear that if I try to, that I will inevitably overlook someone, and I do not wish to do that.

Most of all for Edna your voice is at last being heard in spite of the law and system that tried to bury the truth.

Introduction
Why You Need to Read This Book

Chapter One
The Current Law. Why Whistle-blowing Law Has Failed

Chapter Two
Complicit In Compliance. The Vested Interests That blight
Whistle-blower protection. Evidence from 100 frontline staff

Chapter Three
The Rule of Law. How These Rules Have Been Discarded
Resulting in Injustice.

Chapter Four
Who Is a Whistle-blower. Who is NOT a Whistle-blower

Chapter Five
What is The Public Interest. The Ground-breaking Definition
That Ensures Only The Genuine Are Protected.

Chapter Six
Why EU Whistle-blowing Law will Fail. The Reliance On
Competent Authorities To Investigate.

Chapter Seven
IN-Competent Authorities. How these authorities have failed
and will continue to fail

Chapter Eight
Edna's Law The Qualifying Disclosures. Including Edna's
Law
Recommendations for The Official Secrets Act.

Chapter Nine
The 13 Steps. The First Law with an Inbuilt Scrutiny System

Chapter Ten
Summary

Introduction

When a law goes through Parliament it is amended by those who either have no real understanding of the issues involved or even more worrying, those who have vested interests in big business.

Therefore, I put the case for Edna's Law before those who have most to gain by its full implementation, you the public. Whistle-blowers need Edna's Law so they can protect **you**. If you have ever watched the news and asked, **how can this happen?**

. Gosport Memorial Hospital
. Orchard View
. The thousands of children abused and failed by the authorities across the UK
. Winterbourne View
. Mid Staffs
. Hillsborough
. Why does it take years to expose cover-ups, failures, injustice and corruption.

This is the book you need to read

This book is both a wake-up call and a call to arms.

I write this book as someone who has experienced first-hand what happens to those who speak out and try to stop abuse and serious wrong-doing.

I have witnessed the horrific torture that can be inflicted on defenceless people like Edna and how those with the power to act, choose to protect themselves and their organisations' reputation, no matter what the cost. If you think there are systems in place to protect the vulnerable, Whistle-blowers and the public from harm, then the factual evidence contained in this report will shock and alarm you.

Most people would automatically stand up for their own rights and fight for their loved ones if need arose. What makes a Whistle-blower so different is that they fight to protect people that are not their family, people who they may well not even know, and they do so at great cost to themselves. The Whistle-blower's action to protect you and your loved ones is the kindness of a stranger you did not even notice if you are lucky. But all too often the Whistle-

5

blower and the vital message they carry are left to sink
without a trace by a hostile and accountability-averse
system. Until the day the accident happens, when the
disaster results in loss of life, or the years of continual abuse
are finally exposed decades later, it is only <u>then</u> the public
ask how could this happen?

You will often hear the term "the public interest" used, for
example:
It is in the public interest to prosecute/not prosecute a case.

It is in the public interest to publish this story

What is the **crucial** difference between the Whistle-blower
acting in the public interest and **all** those others who make
decisions on public interest issues?
The Whistle-blower is **not paid** to make that decision; **it is
not part of their job**, it is an act **without** self-interest, but it
can all too often be an act that results in financial hardship. It
costs the Whistle-blower to take such an action.
I have defined a ground-breaking definition of all the
elements involved in the essence of whistle-blowing in the
public interest. My definition, which is based on evidence
and experience, openly challenges **every** academic belief
and legal precedent so completely that it shakes the
foundations of all whistle-blowing law.
Edna's Law is the first whistle-blowing law that resets the
boundaries on the side of both the genuine Whistle-blower
and the good employer.
Every Time a Whistle-blower is ignored and then forced from
their job, it sends a clear message to all; **keep quiet or you
will be next.** This allows abuse to continue unchecked
because Silence is why all abuse continues and what feeds
that silence are Ignorance, Complacency and Denial.
Every day in the court's judges need to ask what was
intended by certain legislation. The aim of this book is to
ensure that no judge will ever ask that question of Edna's
Law because there will be no doubt as to my intentions.
When a Whistle-blower reports genuine concerns to their
employer and their employer fails to act, regardless of
whether those concerns relate to criminal or other forms of
wrong-doing, it is **the failure to act** that becomes a criminal

offence. Good employers have nothing to fear from Edna's Law because unlike the current law, Public Interest Disclosure Act (PIDA), Edna's Law only protects the genuine Whistle-blower.

This book does not consist of the usual 30 pages of legal jargon but includes compelling evidence in support of Edna's Law.

The key aims of Edna's Law

. To ensure vulnerable people like Edna are immediately protected

. To ensure the public interest is served

. For the first time to have a whistle-blowing law that complies with the "rule of law"

. To protect Whistle-blowers from all detriment, including future detriment

. To ensure only genuine Whistle-blowers are protected.

To stop employers/accountable persons from covering up wrong-doing, tampering with or destroying evidence

. To stop employers causing detriment to Whistle-blowers

. To make blacklisting in all its forms a criminal offence

. To treat gagging orders and mediation as attempts to pervert the course of justice

. To protect Whistle-blowers from all workplaces equally and not discriminate against any Whistle-blower

. That no protected person has to battle the system for years to obtain justice but instead is guaranteed transparency and accountability as a legal right

. **To ensure that those who disclose information in exchange for financial or other personal gain are <u>not</u> protected by Edna's Law and <u>not</u> afforded the status of Whistle-blower**

. **To ensure all decisions to prosecute or not, are based on the evidence, <u>all</u> the evidence and nothing <u>but</u> the evidence**

I can see no logical reason why a law cannot be written in clear and plain language. **Edna's Law is a people's law** and therefore is written in plain English.
A law supported by the people, for the people cannot be ignored by any Government. Edna's Law has to be implemented **in full** and cannot be amended by vested interests. There should only be one interest involved and that is **the public interest.**

Chapter One
The Current Law

The law that is currently failing Whistle-blowers, The Public Interest Disclosure Act 1998 or PIDA.

PIDA has completely failed to recognise, capture or define the genuine Whistle-blower or the essence of "the public interest" in relation to this issue and as a consequence has been widely misused and misinterpreted, which serves no-one, least of all the public interest.

The first Whistle-blowers to use PIDA, The BUPA 7, were completely failed by a law which was never competently drafted and was allocated for use in Employment Tribunals, a court setting that is judicially sub-standard and which has neither the powers to hear such cases nor the competency to judge such cases. This issue is more fully detailed in the section on the rule of law later in this book.

The story of the first PIDA case The BUPA 7 is told in my book Beyond the Façade.

Whilst the BUPA 7 were the first to be failed by PIDA, it is only fairly recently that Public Concern at Work (Protect PCAW) has conceded that most Whistle-blowers' concerns are ignored.

Public Concern at Work (PCAW) now known as "Protect" who I will refer to as "Protect PCAW" was instrumental in drafting PIDA, a law aimed not at the court room but at employers having whistle-blowing policies and procedures. The main income of the charity, Protect PCAW, comes from selling such policies and procedures to industry.

Protect PCAW maintains that such policies will change culture however this can only be seen as a marketing strategy that is not substantiated by the factual evidence. For every Whistle-blower failed, there are countless lives affected by abuse, suffering, theft, miscarriages of justice, public safety, fraud and many other serious issues.

If policies and procedures changed culture, then would it not be reasonable to expect an organisation to improve its culture where Whistle-blowers have exposed wrong-doing? The BUPA 7 case exposed widespread abuse of defenceless vulnerable people in 1999. *See Breaking the Silence part 3, to fully understand the culture that any effective Whistle-blowing law must overcome. The evidence of those abused in other BUPA homes since 1999 is an indictment of PIDA.

The below extract is from a judge's criticism of BUPA's whistle-blowing policy, 16 years after the BUPA 7 case. When an organisation is entrenched in a culture of denial and Whistle-blower smearing such as BUPA is, there is not a whistle-blowing policy in the world that would be fit for purpose. Such policies are paper exercises in such organisations, perversely those very organisations where Whistle-blowing is most crucially needed.

In October 2015 Pamela Wolfendon was jailed for systematic abuse of vulnerable people. Judge Davis said,

"*You believed you were able to do as you pleased - there was no-one else in authority, the residents were unable to complain, the staff were frightened of reprisals if they protested.*"

He criticised the whistleblowing procedures as unfit for purpose as they failed to allay the fears of staff recrimination should complaints be made about those in authority.

Compassion in Care has nothing to gain from the protection of Whistle-blowers, we are not compromised by any conflict of interest and will never be part of the self-serving gravy train that sees Whistle-blowers as a money-making opportunity. The next chapter deals with this issue in full.

Chapter Two
Complicit in Compliance
Proposed Law Changes

Why Whistle-blowers are being failed by proposed law changes and how the Parliamentary system has been hijacked by unscrupulous lobbyists.

Compliance

The enemy of whistleblowing protection

One of the first things I learnt as a whistle-blower is that whistleblowing policies and procedures do not protect you.

In my first book Beyond the Facade I refer to policies and procedures only being of use *"if I had stuffed them under my clothes to protect me when I had been hit with a chair by an angry staff member"*.

Since then I have learnt so much more, all of which confirms my original instinct.

Policies and procedures on whistle-blowing are the product of the compliance industry, which is a multibillion-dollar sector. Whilst those hawking compliance- friendly law are raking in profit, whistle-blowers continue to be completely failed by such laws.

COMPLICIT IN COMPLIANCE

There is an insidious circle of individuals whose names appear again and again on the gravy train passenger list.

Firstly, the charity that was formally known as **PCAW**, and has since changed its name to "**Protect**", drafted the UKS current whistleblowing law, The Public Interest Disclosure Act (PIDA). This act heavily relies on employer compliance.

PIDA was a complete failure from the first case as it was never robust enough to be used in a court setting and certainly not in an employment tribunal setting. It was written for the purposes of compliance and the incorrect presumption that industry compliance offered the protection whistle-blowers needed.

Protect PCAW's, main income is from selling compliance packages to employers. They are currently backing EU compliance industry-friendly whistle-blowing law. Billions will be made across the EU by such companies, but alas the cost will be that whistle-blowers will still not be protected.

Protect PCAW are also pushing forward on *a law here that would make compliance mandatory as well as extremely lucrative for **Protect PCAW**.

The All-Party Parliamentary Group (APPG) on Whistle-blowing, run by WBUK.

WBUK are an organisation whose only objective is to make money out of vulnerable whistle-blowers. When there is no profit in a case, no support is given.
This organisation is completely compromised and has caused nothing but harm to whistle-blowers.
We have published *extensive evidence on **WBUK**; please see www.compassionincare.com for all evidence referred in this book.

*The Halford Hallmark of Deceit
*The Misconduct of WBUK
*Questions to Government
*WBUK and the APPG Scandal
*The Scandal Behind UK Whistleblowing Law
*Response to Whistleblowing Debate
*https://compassionincare.com/complicit-compliance

Please note also that the CEO of **WBUK, Georgina Halford Hall**, is not a whistle-blower. **WBUK, Halford Hall** and the **APPG on Whistleblowing** are funded by the US law firm **Constantine Cannon**, whose UK branch is headed by **Mary Inman*** *https://www.youtube.com/watch?v=QoY6FEEeTNI

Constantine Cannon are pro the US bounty hunting system, a system that makes this firm massive money in the US. **Constantine Cannon** have lobbied UK Governments for some time to introduce this reprehensible practice to UK law. I will cover the issue of bounty hunting more fully in a later chapter but must stress that bounty or incentives are not whistleblowing.

The US system also includes "**The Office for the Whistle-blower**" an exercise in PR which just adds another useless layer of regulators to oversee the useless regulators that fail to act on whistle-blower's concerns.

We cover the failures of regulators such as the CQC and Safeguarding comprehensively later.

The proposed Law for the Office for the Whistle-blower is currently in the process of going through Parliament. We are doing all we can to alert MPs to the consequences of endorsing a law that will condemn whistle-blowers to yet more injustice, but which will also inevitably condemn those whose lives depend on a whistle-blower speaking out to stop continued suffering.

Norman Lamb MP resigned publicly from the **APPG on Whistleblowing** when the CEO of **WBUK** refused to be transparent about funding.
Meanwhile **Baroness Susan Kramer** is currently pushing for "The Office For The Whistle-blower" via a private members bill. **Baroness Kramer** is on the record as pro bounty hunting and has even recently appeared on the same platform as **Bradley Birkenfield**, whom both **WBUK** and **Baroness Kramer** consider to be a Whistle-blower, when he is definitely not a Whistle-blower.

The views and agendas of the above individuals will make the word Whistle-blower synonymous with greed and self-interest. The aim of this book is to clearly shine a light on the essence of public interest and by doing so enable the genuine whistle-blower to be recognised as such. Therefore, enabling the polar opposite of Whistle-blower to be equally recognised for what they are.

Edna's Law does not rely on a system that has continually failed, or on regulators who have rated the worst hospitals and care homes as good whilst subsequent scandals proved otherwise.

Over 90% of helpline calls received by the Compassion in Care helpline are serious concerns about care homes rated "good" by the CQC.

Safeguarding asks care homes to investigate themselves and they inevitably find themselves not guilty. If this same system was applied to criminal cases the prisons would be empty.

CQC only rate homes bad when the harm has been done and CQC have been told about it.

To stop harm, it is futile and complacent to rely on a regulator, because any law that relies on a regulator to investigate whistle-blower's concerns is both fatally flawed and criminally complacent and "**The Office for The Whistle-blower**" is exactly such a law.

I called the UK offices of **Constantine Cannon** posing as a potential client, a care home whistle-blower seeing widespread physical and emotional abuse. This situation would have no value in the US bounty system as it did not involve fraud or a gain to the US Government, who only pay bounty for convenient information. The response I got confirmed my worst suspicions. I put these facts to **Mary Inman** of **Constantine Cannon** whose response to these unsavoury truths can be viewed in the below video*

*https://www.youtube.com/watch?v=QoY6FEEeTNI

Protect PCAW have endorsed **WBUK** and the recommendations of the **APPG on whistleblowing** which were written by **WBUK**.

Navex Global are a multinational compliance company who make millions from whistleblowing compliance.

Navex Global endorse and support the recommendations of the **APPG on whistleblowing**.

Navex Global also generously fund the organisation **WBUK**.

As with all my work I let those on the front line, whistle-blowers and potential whistle-blowers speak for the protection that compliance procedures have in the real world.

The Reality of Compliance

Evidence from The Front Line

All of the below comments are from front line staff, they all refer to just one company, this demonstrates beyond question the level of toxic corporate culture any effective whistle-blowing law must be able to confront. Some of the below comments are from whistle-blowers who have contacted our helpline, and some are from a staff review web site. All are anonymized. The deeply disturbing culture that emerges from the below evidence is by no means exclusive to this company.

It is important to note that the company in question uses **Navex Global** for its whistleblowing compliance systems. It is also important to note that **Navex Global** is directly influencing proposed UK whistleblowing law, to add to the injustice, no whistle-blower is afforded the same privilege.

The following cases are all from the last 30 months, they involve 11 different job roles from care home staff to admin and other roles within the same company. Many involve whistleblowing, others demonstrate the culture and barriers to whistleblowing that exist. All helpline cases have informed the relevant authorities, and nothing has been done to address the concerns. These are the same authorities that the proposed "**Office for the Whistle-blower**" would rely on for action. That is why Edna's Law is so different, it is based on the harsh reality that so many in power cannot even grasp; reporting abuse or other concerns is one thing, getting action taken is quite another.

The genuine whistle-blower will often be unfairly labelled "obsessive" when in actual fact it is only the genuine whistle-blower who will continue to fight for the concerns to be addressed long after the original whistleblowing. I think of whistleblowing as not a single step but as a marathon, the more serious the wrongdoing reported the longer the whistle-blower has to fight for action to be taken.

This was summed up by someone involved in the new EU whistleblowing law, who said to me, "*we just need people to whistle blow to stop the wrong*". This could not be further from the reality. Only Edna's Law recognises this key fact and only Edna's Law protects the whistle-blower and stops the wrong-doing they reported.

If you believe that any form of whistleblowing compliance policy will protect Whistle-blowers than read the case snapshots and think again.

If you believe any current regulator can be relied upon to stop abuse and other wrongdoing, then this book will open your eyes to the shocking reality faced by both whistle-blowers and victims' families, there is nowhere to go for accountability. There is no authority willing or capable of investigating at all.

It is important to note that the following 100 case snapshots from this one company were chosen from research that included 1023 cases involving this same company. This is the extent of toxic culture that exists in the worst companies and only Edna's Law recognises this.

One

"I worked there about five years, they brought a new manager in two or three years ago and culture changed, very bad bullying. brought a lot of own people in, care deteriorated, Informed the company and CQC, nothing happened. Then company X brought someone else in recently who has worked all over the area, lots of jobs in short space of time, complete blow up, I left because no good. I see now they are in the papers for bad care Etc, but this has been going on for two years, nothing new. The company and CQC should be ashamed. Lack of manager who knows what they doing, the company don't care about staff or residents, money, money, money"

Two

"X is the worst company I have ever had the displeasure to work for,
Training was ridiculous and contradicting,
Go in on your first day, nobody shows you around, or tells you what to do, they just, go on, get on with it. Your basically thrown into the deep end with no support.
Other carers are so miserable and walk around with a chip on their shoulder, team spirit is not something they are familiar with.
Hot meal? Ha
Breaks are paid but non-existent. I worked at X for a year and got half a lunch break once.
You never ever sit down. You're lucky if your allowed to use the loo. Expect a lot of UTIs because you will be holding it in. Staffing is beyond a joke, 3 carers majority of the time looking after 35 -40 palliative care residents. Hard, hard, work and there is no, thank you, you are doing a great job at the end of it.
The Nurses are lazy. Say good morning or goodnight to the nurses and you're lucky to get a grunt out of them.
Holiday requests are binned, you will have a holiday when the big man says so.
Whistleblowing is encouraged. Yeah if you want to get sacked.

*I witnessed some appalling things at a X home, when I
reported I was threatened. I walked in the end
Don't do it if you want to be a carer, go elsewhere. Don't
slug your guts out for these corporate money grabbing
bigots, no space to write all the cons."*

Three

*"X wrecks lives, there is no person-centred care in this
company. Management look after management. Speaking
up for the residents suffering (although they say they
promote it) is a way to see you out of a job. Very sad! It's the
people you don't want looking after your Mum/Dad/Gran that
will be in this job. Put all the hours god sends in and they
don't say a word, then you'll be fine, if you actually care it will
break your heart!!!"*

Four

*"Whistle-blowing policies oh they have them alright, but blow
the whistle in a X home and you're out the door so quick"*

Five

*"X Terrible place to work company misleads people, training
is useless as it conflicts with what really happens, after
training you are treated like dirt by jumped up cocky
managers who patronise you constantly. If they could chain,
you to a desk this lot would. The company doesn't follow
procedures, tells you when you can be off, yet expect you to
drop everything for them. Excuse after excuse to extend
probation and if there is a chance to get shot of you, they
will. No support for staff who are abused by its members or
internal staff, you're constantly put down in front of people,
even occupational health issues are not discussed privately
or kept confidential. Managers sit at the end of the pods
eating and cackling with other managers and generally doing
FA. Yet staff working are penalised if caught eating or
talking. I was actually reprimanded for being too nice as it
made for long call times, yet in the training the head of
service claims he doesn't care how long a call takes as long
as its customer driven, and the customer is happy. It's a load*

of rubbish if you want a company to undermine U make you feel worthless and generally treat you like a dummy then X is for you. Horrible place to work absolutely horrible and put any thoughts that you will be able to get another job whilst working there out of your head, once they have you on those very long tedious shifts, mainly because it cannot keep staff as everyone hates it, you will never get time off when you need it. They even tell you when you can go to the toilet and how long it should take demoralising and demeaning"

Six

"Awful the other staff members who are above you never bothered to resolve any issues which occurred. Other staff members were always rude towards each other, there was no team spirit and was an awful company to work for, although I enjoy care so much and there was absolutely nothing wrong with the residents. The staff are completely and utterly neglecting them and not given them the appropriate amount or level of care therefore leaving them to be in a more vulnerable situation then they are already in. Also, after promising to promote me to a senior care assistant this never happened"

Seven

"Been working for X for a while now, the main problem is money they don't pay well so don't attract quality workers or don't keep them. Typical day busy, rushed, some of the workers are amazing, shame they are not recognised. Hardest part making managers understand the ways and not encouraging any change. Whistle blowing policy is very limited they find out who it is and make people feel bad. They don't value their staff enough and should give credit where credit is due.
 The big name has high expectations which frankly are not met, the home has broken curtains, leaking gutters and dirty furniture and this is not cheap to stay here. Our elderly deserve so much better, I'm so embarrassed when new people look round. All I can do is my job to the best standard

and care for our elderly. They push managers up the ladder quickly and don't support them leaving staff members low and problems occur when complaints arrive, they usually blame the manager, that person leaves and the process starts again, avoid because like me you will get attached and care and find it hard to walk away. CQC don't follow up enough they should it's the only time managers take notice"

Eight.

"Poor patient care, worst management, rude and unhelpful. She didn't have a clue what she was doing fat and lazy and lacked experience. Area manager very young and lacked experience. Issues dealt with very poorly. Nobody for management knows what to do, worse management I've ever come across. All staff are unhappy and unhelpful. x have poor work ethics and are just concerned about how much money they are making.
Not treated as a valued staff member, X do not care for their patients, it's just about meeting targets. X is a glorified NHS practice broken and old equipment. avoid "

Nine

"I started with X in (Date) was told the home I was at was struggling, but they were improving. I asked for days off at one home due to my health and the location of the home, I was given nights at another home.
After a month of consistent bullying by one of the night staff I swapped to days. Day staff were really unwelcoming, like really horrible to you, bar the odd one or 2. They made you think they were your friends then knife you in the back as soon as you were out of earshot, then deny it when caught out.
I was told the staff think you get very stressed, when the reason I was always so stressed was the fact I was practically managing a unit of 26 residents, short staffed with no senior and nurses who didn't give a monkeys, doing most of the stuff myself, bar hoisting. Forced By unit managers to do things with residents I was uncomfortable with, i.e.

shower a resident with an agency carer who was less than capable, when the service user had just been served notice due to his levels of challenging behaviour.

I witnessed and reported abuse several times nothing done, was accused by one of the more abusive ones myself. So, the manager tried to force me to swap units to somewhere I would have been uncomfortable general palliative care. I ended up signed off for 3 weeks because of anxiety before I started my new job.

Always short-staffed manager knew how to blackmail me into agreeing to cover nights when I was on days. asked me at least once a week then because of all the silly swapping and changing he'd asked me to do complained I was short of hours..."

Ten

"One of the worst set ups I have ever encountered, understaffed undervalued, fantastic people doing great work for a pittance in extremely trying circumstances...X is a scandal and its everywhere someone is making money"

Eleven

"X Whistleblowing policies? What a joke, they could be written on a stamp, whistle blow? There's the door"

Twelve

"People are frightened to stand up to managers and tell them what they really think, and somehow done by employees who say they have put negative scores, uncannily always say we are happy with our job"

Thirteen

"I have seen What happens to people who whistle blow in this job, they do not have a job anymore I have seen bad things and try to challenge them but I would not go to management and ask to enforce the whistle blowing policy I may as well write out my resignation letter"

Fourteen

"typical day? never enough staff for nursing residents and now the home is under embargo, what have I learned? If you value your pin get out quick…. This is not a rant by a bitter ex-employee, it's from a nurse who has worked in the NHS for many years and just happens to love the older generation….. There appears to be the same theme running through most reviews which really should not be 3 star, we love our residents, but X are an appalling company to work for"

Fifteen

"It's like banging your head against a brick wall, there is appalling abuse in this home, if you try to say anything your life is made a misery"

Sixteen

"X tell you when you start working there that whistleblowing is encouraged but you quickly learn when you see bad things happening that keeping your mouth shut is what is encouraged"

Seventeen

"there is a look the other way attitude, things are covered up all the time"

Eighteen

"X terrible company, staffing levels are run on a minimum so as soon as there is sickness or annual leave things go pear shaped, no back up is given 80% of the time you're working short staff, mention this and your fobbed of"

Nineteen.

"underpaid and overworked, unit run on a bums on beds not resident's needs. Senior management are placing unsuitable residents in unit, which is making the work even harder, *clicky as lots of staff come from area and been here years. unit manager is fantastic caring and supportive but banging her head off a brick wall with senior management. building is run down, small rooms, poor decoration, some dubious care, some staff more concerned about time it takes to help with care rather than meeting needs. Baths and showers are a rarity due to time constraints. Staff feel the need to have a certain amount of people up and the same amount in bed for night staff. A blind eye is turned…"*

Twenty.

"I have worked for X a time now and since becoming a senior it has come very apparent that management do not care how under staffed you are, they expect you to complete all the work anyway with no help, no breaks and no extra for braking your back just to get a single days work done. They have no respect for carers or seniors. They cover up or turn a blind eye to any problem i.e. such as lost drugs, bullying in the staffing ranks, if you want to work somewhere where you are valued, don't work for X"

Twenty-One

"My personal experience with X has already made me decide I would never put any of my relatives in a X home because for a typical day there will be only 3 carers on the floor with at least 34 residents to look after and care for. The lack of staff means that the care these people need is not being provided and everything is a rush job except for the paperwork as we are told that is more important, they actually said that to me.
Mix that up with poor management, long hours, terrible pay and with no incentives or bonus schemes and then you would have a pretty good idea what it's like there.
Be careful if you dare to speak your mind because you will end up being bullied by management until you leave "

Twenty-Two

"I have seen 3 members of staff whistle-blow about the same staff members being abusive, those who whistle blew have no job, the abusers are still working here"

Twenty-Three

"The management said, say anything about this and no one will believe you, do you want to lose your job because I know how to deal with troublemakers. People are being abused and that's OK its only saying anything about it that's the problem"

Twenty-Four

"They say all this shit on paper, all the right words about encouraging whistleblowing, but god help you if you open your mouth"

Twenty-Five

"Whistleblowing policies my arse, they are not worth the paper they are written on, try and whistle blow and you're on shit street"

Twenty-Six

"I have worked in care a long time, seen a lot of good and bad things nothing as bad as X, every shift your working so short of staff, some of the staff cut so many corners, there's been so many near misses, people almost dropped from hoists as supposed to be attended by two staff. People always left with no food or drink all day. X is complete shit, so much bullying of staff that try to report bad things, told not to write bad things down just a pack of lies in the paperwork, don't know where to turn"

Twenty-Seven

"X is the worst company to work for, I worked for them a bit over a year. To begin with it was fine, just recently staff have begun bullying, management won't do anything, staff is always short, other day just 4 staff for ** plus residents, the nurses don't do anything, after they have done medication, they sit at the nurse's station all day. When managers told they say sort it out yourself"

Twenty-Eight

"The standards of care are appalling. I attribute this to poor pay which will not attract the decent caring staff you need. Any caring and compassionate individuals will be looking for the door pretty quick. it's not just the care staff that are paid appalling rates for the job they do. The rate for registered nurses is disgraceful, you would keep your sanity and PIN if you worked in a call centre. The company X would put you off nursing for life.

Poor management excessive paperwork which when written up care plans looks great, just a pity that interventions are never put into practice it's just for the inspectors.

Dirty rooms, kitchen staff smoking their lungs off in between preparing meals. Terrible moving and handling, Residents treated like cattle by some inexperienced staff including nurses. Avoid X at all costs, I was lucky to be changing career, the company really needs to improve and pay fairly".

Twenty-Nine

"I have reported the same poor care and abusive staff every time I see what they are doing I report it, Management do nothing just look at you as if you are being fussy, this is dreadful it's a wall of silence, you think the words are coming out of your mouth but no one in this company choses to hear you, as for CQC there useless worse than useless"

Thirty

"If you care about the people then you are treated like you have a performance issue, if you say anything about the completely shoddy care, the hostility from management is hard to bear"

Thirty-One

"At first, I was reporting these incidents of abuse, I actually began to think it was me, that it was the way I was explaining what I saw and that's why no action was taken. Now I know it would not matter how many times I whistle blew or how well I did it, it was always going to fall on deaf ears, I went to CQC nothing happened"

Thirty-Two

"Constantly working with not enough staff and when we told management about this nothing was ever done, and we seemed to get ignored. The lack of support and the amount of pressure that was put on us as a unit was lowering the atmosphere. You'd often go onto a shift where people would tell you they're unhappy and didn't want to be there. Working there was mentally and physically draining, staff would often get moved around not offering stability, I often sensed there was a lot of favouritism going on some staff members could get away with a lot more than others"

Thirty-Three

"Home is abusive when I arrived on shift saw staff pushing residents over, No good from this home sadly, even recently failed CQC inspection! Dangerous place"

Thirty-Four

"Not a nice place to work, hate working here, managers are nasty do not treat staff with respect, you are just a number. Cannot talk to manager without them targeting you"

Thirty-Five

"Bad practices being overlooked. Staff shortages meant that care was becoming a Health and Safety violation every day. Stress levels of all caring and nursing staff was high continually. I reported this site to CQC as trying to care adequately became impossible to accomplish, staff often asked to work double shifts which resulted in mistakes being made, all staff missed breaks regularly to ensure care was given"

Thirty-Six

"X don't follow what they say their homes are about. They make you work at hard staffing levels.
Area managers don't even know your name. X push as much as possible onto the care team. When you raise a concern, you are threatened with warnings"

Thirty-Seven

"I hate going to work it breaks your heart seeing people treated so badly, every time you report the abusive incidents you know you are a little closer to losing your job, it's not safe here for the residents nor for the staff who care and have told CQC that's the end of it for me, knowing that there's no one willing to act everything the home says it treated like gospel by CQC"

Thirty-Eight

"Appalling place to work, staff get treated like dirt. The pay for what the job entails is disgusting. The food is vile, they treat the residents badly making them do things they don't want to do, and force feed them. They hardly ever have the right equipment. Overall a soul-destroying place to work"

Thirty-Nine

"Feels like the company are far more interested in money and protecting their own interests than providing holistic high-quality care"

Forty

"Worked for X for 4 years, company itself is rubbish. It's all about the money coming in and not the residents or staff. Management do not support their staff when many times they have been asked for support. No teamwork and staff getting away with it and no actions were taken… they don't take into consideration staffing levels and resident's needs…."

Forty-One

"If you get offered a job with X run, if you take the position remember you will be swimming with sharks, especially management. Nice home until X took over. Bullied and they lie if you speak up and not what they want to hear, look for another job as they will make your life unbearable. X policies a joke not for the staff only X self-interest"

Forty-Two

"X a vile company to work for, management a disgrace, never there always on holiday, staff are always calling each other or leaving new starters on their own. X only care about paperwork always understaffed not enough carers or nurses, pay is disgusting. Management not approachable were there issues or concerns raised. X only care about how the home looks, don't work for them"

Forty-Three

"Terrible management, very poor organisation, lack of materials, bedding proper cleaning products etc. procedures not always followed, health and safety hygiene etc. friendly but wary co-workers. Break out of scabies kept quiet and staff warned to keep quiet. Residents not always treated with good care and respect. Very hard work not always opportunities to learn further skills, avoid working for X at all costs, lack of staff being valued"

Forty-Four

"...It's not about care at all, it's just fill in the paperwork and leave people calling for help because you are too busy filling in the paperwork, tell CQC about all the dreadful things happening, what do CQC do? Come in and look at the bloody paperwork and say everything is great because the paperwork says so"

Forty-Five

"I hate working here, morale is dreadful, you cannot raise any concerns in a workplace where there is so many serious concerns, it can only get worse"

Forty-Six

"I reported to the regulator not a single issue has changed, I feel gutted and wondered why I bothered to care no one else does"

Forty-Seven

"The CQC are useless, the home just said it's not true and the CQC believed them, it breaks my heart because people are suffering and there is nothing more I can do, there is no one to go to"

Forty-Eight

".... Loyal staff are not valued. concerns for residents are only answered when they become a real danger and residents known to complain or make a fuss to head office are given special over treatment over the others. When staff are unhappy X is fine about letting them leave rather than fixing the problem and as such the turnover rate is really high and every few months the majority of staff have cycled out, the positives about working for X are the staff are really pleasant and work well besides from management and the residents are lovely..."

Forty-Nine

"Appalling, understaffed, undervalued, management did not listen to serious concerns reported. Incidents swept under the carpet. Staff morale rock bottom as everyone was shattered but constantly called on days off to cover sickness. Hardly any time to spend with residents due to poor staffing levels. Managers only concern is the paperwork had to be filled out, they aren't bothered if people have had a drink or turned on time as long as the paperwork said they have. No time to give proper care, I would never work for X again"

Fifty

"X shocking to work for management do not listen to complaints and all efforts to change situations are wasted"

Fifty-one

"Too Much Paperwork and no care, concerns never written down, go to CQC and they go and inspect the paperwork and say all is brilliant in this home when its dreadful. It's awful you spend all the time dreading the next bad thing you are going to see knowing there's no one who is bothered about it"

Fifty-Two

"You won't question anything, if its bad practice shut your eyes and mouth, if you report it look for another job. Head office will cover everything up for management. Staff are vanishing from the place like a rainbow…"

Fifty-Three

"Avoid at all costs the worst company to work for no support from manager all she cared about is interior and how things looked, instead of the care side. double standards sickness was terrible understaffed all the time first week on shift worked on my own because of sickness… a lot of bullying, targeting certain People. Made issues about situation that

were so petty, unit managers don't do anything, apart from bickering in the office and go for plenty of cig breaks more than they are entitled to"

Fifty-Four

"Bad management, senior managers lie and hold information from the CQC and social workers. understaffed overworked. too high expectations from all staff, do not follow their own values. staff are told to hide mistakes and keep concerns from other agencies. only interested in money"

Fifty-Five

"The worst company I have ever worked for, the policies of the way staff/residents should be treated is dated. Long hours and very short breaks and management who ignore your concerns about nursing staff"

Fifty-Six

"People are not fed or given drinks most days, it worries me because people will die, management ignore you and are really vicious to you. I have reported to the CQC, but they looked at the care home's records, and they were all filled in, so they said people were safe, but I know they are not safe. What are you supposed to do? I cannot stay here and watch this happening "

Fifty-Seven

"I did not enjoy my experience with X. I had high hopes after hearing what an established company they are, only to find they are poorly managed, understaffed and the atmosphere was not good.
Staff morale was very low, and I felt I did not receive proper training to do my job. I saw my manager about my concerns and instead of it being in confidence, she passed it on to my line manager, who was a bully and expected everything to be perfect straight away. hardly anytime with the residents as paperwork comes first"

Fifty-Eight

"Avoid if you can, terrible working environment. Management are notorious throughout X homes for their bullying and horrible work ethic. They bully staff into leaving and breach their own policies to fire staff"

Fifty-Nine

"As long as you can turn a blind eye then you will fit in, me of course didn't and therefore had to leave as I choose to work to my job description by keeping residents safe"

Sixty

"Terrible. Management and higher don't care about residents. Whistle blowing reported multiple times, but nothing done. Paperwork faked. threatened with being sacked if I didn't comply, got sacked and reported everything to CQC"

Sixty-One

"An absolute joke. worked for X for one year. The management are an absolute joke, gossip is rife, and they have no understanding and there is zero support. The worst company I have ever worked for. The only pro to working there was the residents and their families. Management speak to members of staff very rudely, favouritism throughout and constant backstabbing. You need a thick skin to work here. I wouldn't let them look after a goldfish let alone a family member"

Sixty- Two

"Whistle blew about risks and abuse to X and to CQC waste of time, the only action that resulted was me being pushed out of the job that I loved"

Sixty-Three

"X values its managers and UTs managers only, particularly in the recruitment department where you only progress if you suck up to the right people. Processes are rarely followed, and the business is not honest or open…"

Sixty-Four

"In the Care home that I worked at I found it really unprofessional in all aspects. Members of staff answering their mobiles to take personal calls whilst looking after patients. There was a general don't care kind of attitude, being the newest member of staff and youngest, I got no support from fellow carers and management staff. I found myself asking questions all the time being new, I was made to feel that I was annoying them by asking.
On several occasions I voiced my concerns to them only to be told in a roundabout way to get on with it. too many so-called managers appearing and disappearing daily, no routine and the staff used to tippex out shifts they didn't want on the roster and change it to suit them. I hated it here and couldn't wait to leave it almost put me off the care profession"

Sixty-Five

"Residents are treated poorly and left for long periods of time. Staff overworked and poorly treated. Absolute waste of time, do not bother getting a job here was extremely disappointing would never let any family be cared for in an X home after this"

Sixty-Six

"I reported abuse to X they did nothing, went to CQC they did nothing, had to leave the home because there was very bad attitude against me after speaking out, there is nowhere to raise concerns if you want action taken, you could scream your head off there's no one listening"

Sixty-Seven

"There is plenty of X paperwork saying how things are meant to be done but it's all a lie, whistleblowing policies and what's supposed to happen, it's all fiction, they come down on you like a ton of bricks if you dare report anything"

Sixty-Eight

"Some of the other Staff I spoke to about the abuse said don't report it you will be forced out, I had to report it though because it was so wrong, what was happening. I stupidly thought it would not cost me my job, but that's exactly what happened and the abuse? I have been told it's still happening"

Sixty-Nine

"Poor management they don't listen to requests such as days off as mentioned in interview stage. Horrible working hours ideas and requests get put forward in meetings and nothing ever gets put in place by management team not treated well as a member of staff"

Seventy

"Paperwork led, I found X to be very paperwork lead and task orientated, paperwork appeared to be more important than giving good quality care to the residents. There were some very good care assistants but there were very poor ones too, when management were informed, they just brought in more paperwork. I found that they pressurised staff into working extremely long hours and I personally found this unacceptable. Call bells were ignored constantly this was something that I had never come across in all my years of working in the care environment. I found their induction training was good it is just a shame that this does not seem to be implemented in the care home"

Seventy-One

"Very disgusting place to work, atrocious management, no respect for anyone. Over worked and underpaid all they want is the paperwork done. The management is vile not caring at all would never recommend them at all"

Seventy-Two

"Worked for X in (Non care role) everything was good at first its only when you see something of concern and express that concern, that is when the nightmare begins"

Seventy-Three

"X promotes amazing values, talks the talk but does not walk the walk. The residents are beautiful but it's not worth the emotional mental and physical exhaustion, stress. The unpaid overtime, well underpaid in all sectors, they do not value employees a lot of turnover and a petty work culture and unfair demands on those that pour their heart and soul into the role and then their efforts are ignored or dismissed. A lot of micromanaging and belittling terrible communication "

Seventy-Four

"I felt like I was being brainwashed I lasted all of 3 months maybe I wasn't cut out for the culture I found myself in and was too customer orientated. Despite constantly receiving good reviews during training and scoring high there was always a reason given to prevent me from moving forward out of the training academy. Was this because I am an older person and didn't fit in with the young vibrant workforce? I'll never know.
Everything is time orientated to the minute, toilet breaks, lunch, blowing your nose etc.
I was told off for being on the phone too long with a client who had discovered she had cancer.
I went for a break and was stopped by a manager who wanted to discuss something (work issue) I didn't manage to get my break and returned to my desk 2 minutes late and

was told to take only 8 minutes for my next break instead of 10 to make it up. I felt like a hamster in a cage on a spinning wheel unable to jump off"

Seventy-Five

"Just a disgrace ...management don't bother about that residents are not cared for the way they deserve to be, honestly, we do try, we can only do the best with what we have and it's not good enough. Don't work here or put a loved one in here you will not get the respect or the care you deserve, incompetent "

Seventy-Six

"Avoid at all costs, X like to give an image of being in the care industry. All X care about is making money. What kind of healthcare company doesn't pay sick pay? The worst paying care company out there, do your homework you're worth so much more.
We have a regional manager, when she inspects the home, she has no nursing or care experience, she is business orientated, only cares about filling beds and making money. Looks down on all staff, she is unapproachable, uncaring, cold and dismissive of everyone. She insists on staff doing jobs that are not in their job description, long hours, unpaid breaks, short staffed, everything is bad"

Seventy-Seven

"X don't follow their own policies and procedures and when you say this to them, their attitude is just so what?

Seventy-Eight

"The clients and families are wonderful, but the company doesn't care about staff or clients the needs of clients are not met due to poor staffing levels and very poor training. Not only are the clients in a vulnerable position so are the staff. No support from managers and no acknowledgement for going that extra length. poor rates of pay for a massive

company. Furniture and accessories are either broken or smell. There are better companies around please beware "

Seventy-Nine

"X is a large and trusted brand name; the reality of working here is very different. They do not respect the clinical staff that work there and look at staff as numbers and not people. Do not be fooled into working here, the ethical implications of the corporate nature and clinical work are high and are a matter of clinical governance.
Expectation to answer call after call without reflection time or time to complete case notes. The team was fantastic but working flexi shifts for poor money, allowed no time for work life balance or private practice.
I've moved to a smaller local company who value counselling and understand the need for self-care and quality of therapeutic contact. Bad management, poor communication between departments and no respect for staff"

Eighty

"There is a really bad atmosphere all the time, half the staff abusing or neglecting the residents and the other half struggling for caring about what is happening, the management support the abusive staff, the good staff are told if you don't like it, there is the door, lots of good staff leaving"

Eighty-One

"X management disgusting, reporting concerns loads of times, nothing done, went to CQC, they just listened to X management and take their word all is good, it's so frustrating, I don't know who is worse, X for covering up or CQC for believing bullshit"

Eighty-Two

"Shocking, hard and stressful, no one cares about anything, unhappy residents. Management don't care or have any

*concern for your health and expect you to work when you
are ill and put residents at risk.
Management gave me warnings for nothing they just wanted
me to leave. Management tells you not to be anyone's
friend, residents and staff. Change your shifts for more liked
staff and won't tell you. Most new staff don't manage their
first shift, no help, no training"*

Eighty-Three

*"Management are dreadful bullies, they make your life a
misery if you raise a single concern about poor care, they
are on your back all the time. No matter how bad the things
you are reporting are, they don't want to know and tell you to
get on with your job"*

Eighty-Four

*"Management are rude and there's no discretion at all.
You're made to feel like you're nothing and spoken to like
you can't do anything good or right. Especially when you
been there long time. Low wages no sick pay, although
given hours you're more likely to work over that, so basically
you work yourself to death and get no thanks for it. For a
health company worst I have ever known, there are no
benefits from it at all apart from stress and illness. The only
good thing is the employees are lovely to work with and the
residents are lovely to work with, I used to love my job
before X came along"*

Eighty-Five

*"I reported serious concerns about abuse, those who did the
abusing were protected, I was treated like the bad one for
reporting them. X Management bully and shout at you till you
can't face it anymore and leave"*

Eighty-Six

*"It's a lovely place to work and a rewarding job and I would
still be happy working there if I had not witnessed abuse and
reported it. That's when you see a very different company,*

when there is abuse that's when you see how shit a company like X is"

Eighty-Seven

"Started well, I was thrilled to get this job - it was completely different to anything I'd previously done and now had the opportunity to look after sick children. Shortly after being taken on as full-time day staff, I was put onto permanent nights.no real choice in the matter, it's just that the only packages they had in the area I lived were night cover. Managers were increasingly hard to get hold of, and not very helpful when you did speak to them. If I ever had to use the on-call service overnight, due to a query about my patient, bear in mind I was working with tracheostomies, life support etc and I'm NOT a nurse. I always felt as though I was inconveniencing the nurse on call. Training was good in some parts but horrendous in others, I went a whole year of caring for one patient, with inadequate training, having been completed. The managers always said they'd get around to it but never did"

Eighty-Eight

"The Manager was useless didn't care about staff or residents, she should never of managed a care home. Most of the staff were backstabbing and hypocrites, my advice stay away from X, receptionist always leaked out confidential information"

Eighty-Nine

"Do not work there, worst job I ever had!!!!
Disgusting pay, diabolical manager, no flexibility. Loads of lies to protect the management. No one listens in higher management. Also overpriced for the care given. Would rather be un-employed then work for X and will never see a relative of mine in there"

Ninety

"X are only in for the money. Very poor management throughout the company. Wages are very low compared to other companies. No support within your job status, poor management, poor laundry assistants, no support when needed very unclean"

Ninety-One

"{ Management said to me about a week after I had been there, think they saw how shocked I was at what I was seeing, they said don't even think about whistleblowing, believe me you will regret it, keep your head down and get on with your job, never mind what other people are doing. It's the worst place I ever worked, I feel like crying most days and do sheds tears after shift. Some of the good staff told me lots of people have been pushed out after going to CQC or council"

Ninety-Two

"A hugely protracted and convoluted product, and a company that no longer resembles nor serves its original purpose. Member services advisers train to (push back). (Sic) With an introduction to the company consisting of a warning of speaking badly upon expulsion. Vulgar revolving door employment policy, not able to sustain or stem the mass exodus of both employees and members alike. Top down intimidation and complete absence of autonomy"

Ninety-Three

"Everyone knew I had whistle blown, management had told them I was complaining that staff were lazy, staff were really hostile to me, I tried to explain it was abuse I reported and only some staff, but they believed manager. That's how they get people who care out, they tell the staff a pack of lies and they do the dirty work for the manager"

Ninety-Four

"Awful, don't go there you would be better off out of work than working for X. Management have no idea and the last thing they do is care. Staff on the floor usually care and try hard but get dragged down by the management"

Ninety-Five

"X their attitude is there is nothing wrong with leaving people hungry and thirsty, neglected, suffering abusive people shouting and frightening them, there is nothing wrong at all with any of that, there is only something very wrong with reporting it"

Ninety-Six

"*Over worked, underpaid, exhausting, low staff morale, lack of support, total chaos, no one knows what they are doing including management* "

Ninety-Seven

"Issues like very bad care, abusive staff also work there who have been there a long time and been reported many times before, it's a joke, whistleblowing about staff who are dangerous abusers and all that happens is they get put on training courses and then start abusing again, CQC are there to help X coverup"

Ninety-Eight

"I have worked in care a long time and seen good and bad but nothing like this, you tell CQC and the council and they don't care, X just cover it up, you're completely on your own"

Ninety-Nine

"X management only care about money and covering up what is going on. The attitude is, oh people being badly abused, that's ok. They keep saying they will deal with it, but

nothing happens, I said I would report them to CQC, and they just laughed and said there is the phone"

One Hundred

"X They don't care about abuse or people suffering, they don't care about whistle-blowers because there is nowhere to go to get help, there is no one who will listen, CQC are up the arse of X. I am on the side of the residents, but who's on my side?"

Chapter Three
The Rule of Law

There are basic requirements that have to be met in order to comply with the rule of law. I would list the following as what I consider to be crucial elements:

Fair and open disclosure of all evidence
Judgments based on all the evidence
Access to a suitable court
Legal redress
No punishment without crime
Equality of arms
Impartial and suitably qualified judges
Courts which do not exceed their jurisdiction
The safeguard of a jury
Scrutiny

The following short quotes are from "The Rule of Law" by Tom Bingham who held the offices successively of Master of the Rolls, Lord Chief Justice of England and Wales and Senior Law Lord of the UK. He is the only person to have held all three offices.
I found this book to be exceptionally helpful because it defined the rules of justice and those rules were exactly what I thought they should be. This book showed me that the justice I have sought for so long was actually supposed to exist in the first place.

Page 86 *"It is not in the interests of those involved in a dispute or of society as a whole that victory should go to the stronger, in modern terms the party who can send in the best armed heavies"*

Page 87, *describing the following quote of Dr E J Cohn as "Making the case with compelling authority"*
"Legal aid is a service which the modern state owes to its citizens as a matter of principle. It is part of the protection of the citizen's individuality which, in our modern conception of the relationship between the citizen and the state, can be claimed by those citizens who are too weak to protect themselves. Just as the modern state tries to protect the

poorer classes against the common dangers of life, such as unemployment, disease, old age, social oppression etc., so it should protect them when legal difficulties arise. Indeed, the case for such protection is stronger than the case for any other form of protection. The state is not responsible for the outbreak of epidemics, for old age or economic crises but the state is responsible for the law. That law again is made for the protection of all citizens, poor or rich alike. It is therefore the duty of the state to make its machinery work alike, for the rich and the poor"

Taking the issues of access to a Court, Legal Redress and Equality of Arms
in relation to Whistle-blowers, PIDA and Employment Tribunals
The Whistle-blower is currently expected to find the means to obtain legal representation, can be threatened with costs for proceeding with a claim and often is expected to represent themselves.
Edna's Law is based on the evidence gathered from over seven thousand Whistle-blowers who have contacted the Compassion in Care help-line.
These Whistle-blowers were predominantly from health and social care, but I began to see an increasing number of Whistle-blowers from other sectors. We have never turned a Whistle-blower away, so I co-founded the Whistler and I run that help-line also, on which I have been contacted by Whistle-blowers from education, construction, police, probation, finance, prisons and aviation, and retail among other areas.
The sobering reality is that our evidence shows that those who are in the lowest paid jobs are the most likely to witness the worst abuse. PIDA expects the Whistle-blower, whatever their background, at the worst period of financial hardship they are ever likely to experience, to find the financial means to access the alleged protection of this law.
Our evidence also shows that 90% of the Whistle-blowers who contact us cannot access the law at all.
In contrast Edna's Law would protect the Whistle-blower and the vital message they carry. The Whistle-blower would not be expected to finance their own case.

If acting in the public interest does not demand the State's protection, then what does?

Should the Whistle-blower be unable to return to work due to harassment, then at the point a decision is made to proceed to trial, the employer must pay the Whistle-blower's full salary for the remainder of the process. See the legal redress section for full details on this.

In contrast PIDA leaves the Whistle-blower to make an application for interim relief (a legal term most whistle-blowers do not understand) which is rarely applied for given the obstacles and is rarely given in any event.

Section Three: Self Representation or No Win No Fee.

PIDA presumes that the average worker from every industry will have legal training in order to represent themselves. I have sat through enough cases to see the injustice of this. The employer at the very least will have the resources to secure even basic legal representation but they could also be a company with an in- house legal department, public relations team and the resources to secure the very best barristers.

The Whistle-blower is expected to be able to take on all these and be on an equal footing. If you want to see injustice in action attend a genuine Whistle-blower's PIDA case. In effect PIDA guarantees that (in the words of Tom Bingham). "*victory for the best armed heavies*"

On the matter of "no win, no fee" agreements in PIDA cases this is at complete odds with the element of public interest. I have seen this many times and have experienced this as a Whistle-blower myself. When an offer to settle is made by the employer, the Whistle-blower is advised to settle, or the court will hold it against them and if they lose the Whistle-blower will have to pay all legal costs.

It is in a solicitor's interests to obtain their own costs, but it is not in the public interest to have out of court settlements. Edna's Law does not allow for any conflict of interest to impede the public interest.

A law that cannot be accessed is not a remedy but a travesty of justice and what undermines the rule of law is injustice being allowed to stand.

Section Four: Jurisdiction, Impartiality and Disclosure of Evidence

The Rule of law also requires that:

Judges are competent and impartial
Courts do not act beyond their jurisdiction
There is fair and open disclosure of all relevant evidence

As I stated in Section Two of Beyond the Façade once a Whistle-blower is at the stage of needing a legal remedy, then the Whistle-blower and the whistle-blowing can no longer be separated. Whistle-blowing is not just about employment rights and to treat it as such has led to serious injustice and the wrong-doing continuing unchecked. When the law fails the Whistle-blower, it fails all those whom the Whistle-blower was trying to protect.
When employment tribunals were first established, they were intended to be an informal setting whereby the employer and employee could represent themselves. They have developed into a formal court setting with solicitors and barristers representing parties, unfortunately allowing those parties with the financial resources to gain an unfair advantage.
Employment contracts and whistle-blowing policies have taken precedence over the actual whistle-blowing. Edna's Law will remove public interest disclosures from the grasp of HR (human resources) and place such cases where they belong, in a criminal court.
Whistle-blowing cases will often involve judging complex medical, financial or safety issues which employment tribunals do not have the experience or the jurisdiction to judge. They have exceeded their jurisdiction in PIDA cases resulting in judgments that contain perverse, unsound, incompetent and most of all unlawful conclusions.
Employment tribunals are now rightly seen by many as a sub-standard route of redress in the justice system, a matter that requires a full inquiry as a separate issue.
With regard to exceeding jurisdiction. PIDA allows for a Whistle-blower to report concerns of wrong-doing to a prescribed regulator, this looks fine on paper, but the reality

is very different. Instead of being a means to get the wrong-doing addressed PIDA has led to situations of further harm.

The following examples are all factual and are fully supported by documentary evidence:

A judge giving an employer assurances that the prescribed regulator's comprehensive investigation report (which was vital evidence) would not be disclosed during the hearing. This then allowed the employer to proceed with the case that the Whistle-blowers were liars.

Judges who have allowed employers to change their witness statements' evidence mid-way through proceedings and not referred to this in later judgments which went on to conclude that the employer's evidence was credible and consistent when clearly it was nothing of the sort.

Countless cases where the subsequent verdict bears no resemblance to the evidence submitted without any reference to the existence of such evidence.

Countless cases where all the evidence available contradicts the judge's conclusions.

Verdicts where unwarranted and untruthful attacks have been made on Whistle-blower's characters, where the available evidence if used in a case for libel would be successful had the attacks been published by a newspaper instead of in a legal verdict, compounding the Whistle-blowers detriment.

Countless cases where disclosures of serious abuse and wrong-doing were reported to prescribed regulators have resulted in no investigation and no action to stop the abuse and the wrong-doing continuing in spite of Whistle-blowers risking everything to report the concerns.

Countless cases where exceeding jurisdiction should have rendered the verdicts void.

More than 47 Whistle-blowers whose disclosures to the prescribed regulator Care Quality Commission (CQC), resulted in their names being given to their employer by the CQC.

Countless breaches of Whistle-blowers' confidentiality by prescribed regulators

Please see the Compassion In Care website for all our published evidence.

As I said earlier, 90% of Whistle-blowers cannot even access the law's protection at all because of the very reason they need to access the law, because they blew the whistle and are suffering financial hardship as a direct result. PIDA actively discriminates against the very group of people it claims to protect.

The 10% who manage to overcome all the obstacles to access justice are made up of the following:

Those completely failed by PIDA as stated above.

Those who obtain a degree of justice due to being protected by the media coverage.

Those who are protected by PIDA but who are not Whistle-blowers at all.

From the largest section of the 10%, i.e. those completely failed by PIDA and harmed by the law alleged to protect them, very few will survive the further, often insurmountable, barriers to appeal. **An appeal is not a remedy for those verdicts where the only content that is accurate is the name of the judge**.

Appeals can only be on points of law and in those cases where there has been excess of jurisdiction, blatantly biased, incompetent and unlawful conclusions, where all the evidence needs to be re-examined. In effect those verdicts which will not stand up to scrutiny are dealt with in a system where there is no scrutiny to be had.

If whistle-blowing is not a crime, then why does the rule of law allow such treatment and injustice to stand?

These cases are a scar on the face of justice and bring the rule of law into disrepute.

Governments need to protect citizens from sub-standard courts such as Employment Tribunals and from sub-standard laws such as PIDA. Attempts to tinker around the edges are merely adding insult to injury and Edna's Law needs to be implemented in full.

I spoke at "Blacklisting, Bullying and Blowing the Whistle" (organised by the #Blacklisted construction workers) at Greenwich University in September 2016 where Professor David Lewis said that

" PIDA is better than nothing"

My response at the time was: "It could be said that half a rowing boat in the middle of an Atlantic storm is better than nothing. You will still drown but more slowly."

Better than nothing should never be acceptable when applied to a law that is the difference between life and death, safety or suffering for people like Edna.

Tom Bingham says the following on the issues raised by excess of power (pages 61-65 in The Rule of Law):
"A power must also be exercised in a way that, in all the circumstances, is fair, since it is assumed (in the absence of a clearly expressed contrary intention) that the state does not intend to treat the citizen unfairly. It may of course be a vexed question what, in the particular circumstances, fairness requires. But the so called rules of natural justice have traditionally been held to demand, first, that the mind of the decision maker should not be tainted by bias or personal interest (he must not be a judge in his own cause) and, secondly, that anyone who is liable to have an adverse decision made against him should have a right to be heard (A rule of venerability of which is vouched by its Latin version: Audi alteram partem, hear the other party).

The necessary assumption on which to base an argument …that the court must supplement the procedural requirements which the act itself stipulates by implying additional requirements said to be necessary to ensure the natural rules of justice are observed…The decided cases on this subject establish the principle that the courts will readily imply terms where necessary to ensure fairness of procedure for the protection of parties who may suffer a detriment in consequence of administrative action."

Edna's Law will set out exactly what is required of the police, the Crown Prosecution Service (CPS) and the courts, these steps are based on giving the Whistle-blower the right to challenge and for those challenges to be published.
(See the chapter on the 13 steps for full details)
Any decision not to prosecute must justify what evidence was considered,
What evidence was disregarded and why.
Edna's Law draws on the principle of "*Audi alteram partem*", at every step of the way. The Whistle-blower will be given the right to be heard.

All decisions, challenges and independent assessments will be published in full (with identifying information redacted at each stage) as required by the rule of law.

Edna's Law is ground-breaking in its approach and methods of ensuring accountability and fairness from beginning to end.

This is a long overdue method in light of recently exposed miscarriages of justice where the rule of law and public trust have been seriously undermined by a culture of indifference and dishonesty within the administration of justice system.

These cases have included the culture of suppressing vital evidence which would have exonerated innocent suspects had it been disclosed. I will deal with this issue fully in later sections.

Edna's law will not allow evidence to be withheld because "The evidence, all the evidence and nothing but the evidence" is a keystone of Edna's Law, which is the first law in the world with an in-built scrutiny system.

This is because I know that lack of scrutiny is what allows injustice to thrive in the first place and nothing undermines the rule of law more than allowing injustice to prevail.

Tom Bingham Rule of Law page 63-64 Referring to unlawful decisions

"It is an elementary principle that anyone purporting to exercise a statutory power must not act beyond or outside the limits of the power conferred. Here again the principle is so old that it is often known by its Latin name: Ultra vires, beyond the powers.

If judges were themselves to exercise powers which properly belong elsewhere it would be a usurpation of authority and they would themselves be acting unlawfully. As Lord Hailsham pointed out in his 1983 Hamlyn lectures, Thomas Fuller's warning quoted in chapter 1 (Be you never so high, the law is above you) applies to judges no less than ministers."

If this is truly the case, then why has no one been held to account for the many CPS and police actions in suppressing vital evidence or failing to obtain evidence known to exist and vital to a case, which have been exposed in the media?

It seems to me that when it comes to fighting a case of injustice, it is not a question of how right you are and how much evidence you have to prove you are right, but rather a question of how long and how hard you are willing to fight to get the Government to acknowledge the truth.
I could use many examples to demonstrate this but in order to be brief I have chosen the following because Tom Bingham is clear on these points.

Tom Bingham on Disclosure of evidence 68 Rule of Law
"In such cases the judge must decide what evidence to accept and what to reject, must assess the probabilities, must consider any documents and expert evidence that bear on the issue, and must then give his ruling. He must exercise a judgment, not a discretion. Having reached his judgment he has no more discretion than an historian has to decide that King John did not execute Magna Carta at Runnymede in June 1215, when all the evidence suggests that he did"

I agree that when two parties in a case disagree, then any independent expert evidence has to be considered. So, consider the following quote and then apply that concept to PIDA and its statutory prescribed regulators.

Page 61 of The Rule Of Law
"This is important. When Parliament, by statute or statutory regulations, empowers a specific officer (such as a Secretary of State, or the Director of Public Prosecutions or the director of the Serious Fraud Office) or a specific body (such as a housing authority, a social services department, a county council, a health authority, a harbour board or the managers of a mental hospital) to make a particular decision, it does not empower anyone else. It expects that officer or body to follow any guidelines on policy that may have been laid down but expects that the officer or body will exercise his or its own judgment, having regard to any relevant experience and the availability of resources. It does not expect or intend that the decision should be made by some judge who may think he or she knows better. But the presumption is that the decision made will be in accordance

with the law. It is what lawyers call an irrebuttable presumption: one that is conclusive and cannot be trumped"

Except this clearly does not apply to Employment Tribunals in PIDA cases as they can exceed their jurisdiction by rendering the *irrebuttable presumption* null and void.
For example, if a prescribed regulator was, against all the odds, a competent authority and did everything correctly such as the following:
A Whistle-blower reports wrong-doing to his employer and when his employer fails to act, the Whistle-blower goes to the PIDA prescribed regulator who then investigates, upholds the allegations in full and produces an inquiry report detailing the evidence which we will refer to as (Exhibit A). The Tribunal hearing commences, and the employer puts the case that (Exhibit A) should be suppressed as they rebut it and the Tribunal allows this.
When the Whistle-blower receives the verdict, it does not refer to the existence of (Exhibit A) and the Tribunal exceed their powers even further by judging 20 of the disclosures themselves whilst suppressing any reference to the other 100 plus disclosures. The Tribunal have contradicted the prescribed regulator and all the expert evidence in full, including the report of the independent pharmacist.
The Whistle-blower then writes a detailed 30-page response asking the judge to alter his or her conclusions and referring to the 700 pieces of independent evidence including Exhibit A, stating in which bundle, page and paragraph of the judge's copies of the evidence bundles this evidence can be found. The judge completely ignores this.
When does an unlawful act become an illegal act?
When it is challenged, and that challenge is ignored.
Many will say that this could never happen, yet exactly this did happen in the first PIDA case and still is allowed to stand. That is why PIDA is fundamentally failing to protect genuine Whistle-blowers: because it allows the employer to libel Whistle-blowers and rebut the allegedly irrebuttable. PIDA allows judges to act unlawfully - that is how flawed it is. The genuine Whistle-blower not only has to overcome all the barriers to access justice but if they make it to court, they have to fight against the very law that is supposed to protect them in the first place.

Now consider if a judge acted so and the Whistle-blower responded with a detailed written challenge and both these documents had to be published along with the judge's response, would such failures be left to stand? No, they would not and that is why Edna's Law includes a detailed system for such scrutiny.

There is one other issue that needs to be addressed: if a judge commits an unlawful act and usurps the powers of the statutory prescribed regulator and suppresses vital evidence, why is this not considered Misconduct In Public Office and prosecuted as such?

 attention of the Law Commission. Read our full submission Should We Abolish Accountability? on the Compassion In Care website.

 As the rule of law states no-one is beyond the law, is this concept applied to some more than others?

If the rule of law says there can be no punishment without law than it surely must follow that there can be no unlawful act that goes unpunished.

I can only conclude that certain people are above the law because they are not held to account. If we are truly to have trust in the justice system, then we as a country must open our eyes and demand scrutiny and accountability.

The betrayal of absolute trust by authorities such as judges, the CPS and the police needs those responsible held to account.

Edna's Law is the start of upholding the true rule of law, by starting with protection of those who have done the right thing in protecting the public interest and suffered for it.

I would sum up PIDA as follows:

You blow the whistle on something that is true

You have hundreds of witnesses proving it is true

You have hundreds of documents upholding your case

You could even have BBC Panorama film footage

and yet it still would not be enough when your employer demands of the Tribunal that all this evidence is suppressed so that they can publicly call you a liar. The judge says OK and lets this happen, this is PIDA.

Eileen Chubb

Chapter Four
Who is a Whistle-blower?
Who is not a Whistle-blower?

I define a Whistle-blower as the person who speaks out and reports wrong-doing in order to protect others and as a result makes it safe for witnesses and victims to come forward. Please note that this definition refers to three very distinct groups:

The Whistle-blower

The Witness

The Victim

I use the following scenario to explain the crucial difference between these three groups.

Twenty members of staff witness serious abuse at a unit for vulnerable adults. **Three** staff repeatedly report their concerns to their employer who says they will act but when it becomes clear that no action is going to be taken, these three staff then take their concerns to the police.

These three staff are Whistle-blowers.

The vulnerable people being abused are the victims.

During the subsequent police investigation, the remaining **seventeen** staff who witnessed the abuse are interviewed and are assured they will be safe if they give any evidence. **Eleven** staff give witness statements.

These eleven staff are witnesses.

Those are the three groups.

The remaining **six** staff wait until the investigation results in a prosecution that is widely reported in the media resulting in the care home being named and public outrage at the mis-treatment that occurred being made public. It is only then that these six staff post on social media about the abuse they witnessed.

These 6 staff are Sinking Ship Disclosers, NOT Whistle-blowers.

When a Whistle-blower or group of Whistle-blowers report wrong-doing or abuse they are in the hardest place to be and to me the essence of "speaking truth to power" means those who first speak out to someone with the actual power to harm them and who speaks that truth anyway. They are the first over the parapet and they take the full brunt of the anger. They make it safe for others to give witness evidence because the Whistle-blower draws the flak.

The terms Whistle-blower and "speaking truth to power" are currently misused and applied incorrectly to all sorts of situations.

In order to truly understand whistle-blowing in the public interest, Edna's Law alone gets the basics right and clearly defines the elements that identify the genuine Whistle-blower and the essence of acting in the public interest. Edna's Law protects Whistle-blowers by recognising the genuine from the misconceived and the honest from the self-serving.

Every day I witness the extraordinary acts of courage in the face of intimidation, hardship, blacklisting and injustice and this courage needs to be recognised and valued by understanding what the word Whistle-blower truly means.

There are those who abuse and cause harm, the greedy, sadistic and the abusers of power and in the same group are all those who aid and abet the wrong-doing, those who are in a position of power to act but who choose instead to protect their own reputation by attacking the Whistle-blower. There are the Whistle-blowers who risk everything to stop wrong-doing.

The remaining group are everyone else, you the public, people who just live their lives every day oblivious to possibilities such as.

Banks overcharging them.

That someday they or their loved one could be abused and neglected in a care home.

That their loved one could be murdered by someone who was a risk but wrongly assessed when released from prison.

That the train, bus or tram they use every day could be involved in an accident which was totally avoidable.

That they could be spied on by their Government or police.

That their child could be abused by someone in a position of trust who was a known risk.

The list is endless.

The Genuine Whistle-blower

Two examples of genuine Whistle-blowers who refused to walk away and who are typical of all those Whistle-blowers

who contact us or who like Margy Haywood I have met campaigning,
See Margy's interview on Compassion In Care video section
Margy repeatedly reported her concerns about patient care to her employers and the regulator and when no action was taken, she decided to approach BBC Panorama who helped her film the poor care. Margy was subsequently struck off by the NMC for this filming but was reinstated after the public, whose interests she diligently served, gave her overwhelming support. Of course, those who make such disclosures in the public interest are recognised as doing such by the same public.

Karis Le- Winton The Old Deanery, Panorama
Karis contacted the Compassion In Care help-line after she and over a dozen fellow care workers raised concerns about care at the Old Deanery care home in Essex.
They were unable to access PIDA and the lawyer they managed to obtain was in their words, only more focused on possible compensation and not the whistle-blowing, as is common to all such cases and more interested in getting their costs paid by the other side. They never managed to access a court.
Karis contacted Compassion In Care only after going firstly to her employer and subsequently to every single allegedly competent authority, all of whom were equally exposed as negligent in the subsequent scandal and rightly so.
We worked with Karis to get BBC Panorama into the home and they subsequently exposed the abuse that resulted in three workers being jailed.
What should not be forgotten is that it is only the persistence of genuine Whistle-blowers like Karis, who never stop trying to get something done, that stops the wrong-doing. If it were not for this, then those three abusive staff would still be abusing vulnerable people every hour of every day and under the noses of the very authorities who were told about it in the first place and who failed to stop the abuse.

Who Is NOT a Whistle-blower
The Wannabe Whistle-blower

This type would be summed up by the following comments:
"I think abuse is terrible and I have decided to get a job in a care home/hospital so I can blow the whistle".
"I have always wanted to be a Whistle-blower and am going to get a job at xxxx"

"My bunion operation has gone wrong and I am going to blow the whistle about this."

"I think there is bound to be wrong-doing to be uncovered and have applied for a job so I can blow the whistle."
"I have bought under-cover camera equipment and am going to work in xxx places and become a Whistle-blower.
You cannot go to work somewhere in order to be a Whistle-blower this is at odds with the genuine Whistle-blower. No genuine Whistle-blower wants to be a Whistle-blower - they encounter something so bad they are forced to act. If a person goes to work somewhere stating they intend to whistle-blow on what they can find, then prior intent renders any risk of employment detriment null and void. Whistle-blowers speak truth to power; it is not whistle-blowing if speaking truth to someone who has no power to harm you because you never intended to risk anything, and this cannot be bypassed to call yourself a Whistle-blower.
When a wannabe Whistle-blower sets out to find wrongdoing without having any idea what they are looking for, this tainted motivation can harm innocent people.
I have seen social media posts saying, *"I have a comms bag and am going to be a Whistle-blower".*
Alas there are also those who pose as a whistle-blower in order to gain credibility or further an agenda. For example, the CEO of **WBUK Georgina Halford Hall** falsely claims to be a school whistle-blower but is not.

The Sinking Ship Discloser
As I stated in the earlier example these can be staff at a care home who speak out only after the abuse has been exposed, their motivation is to protect themselves or their

reputation, i.e. self-preservation after the harm has been done and has been or is likely to be exposed by others.
A typical example would be the following: M works for a national organisation which is responsible for the safety of particular products. Over time M is aware of a number of unsafe practices, but M never considers whistle-blowing, she makes a few comments about being unhappy but no more. A succession of public scandals follows as a result of avoidable deaths due to these unsafe practices and a formal inquiry begins and then M decides to tell the inquiry what she has known for a couple of years.
The public outrage at her organisation is her motive for doing this as she wants to save herself, being at a senior position in the organisation she will be also held liable. She goes back over minutes of old meetings and she finds several sentences that may suit if she slightly changes the emphasis of what she meant to stress; she is then calls it whistle-blowing retrospectively.
A genuine Whistle-blower would have gone public if need be to save further loss of life.   If you know that lives are at risk, then you do not wait for lives to be lost before speaking out. Edna's Law will have clear procedures to eliminate this type of self-preservation being included as whistle-blowing.

The Walk Away Discloser
This most definitely does not include those genuine Whistle-blowers forced into out of court settlements or gagging orders by PIDA. Edna's Law would ensure they were never in such a position in the first place. These are genuine Whistle-blowers because they need to access the law in the first place.
Genuine Whistle-blowers never walk away after making for example one report but not following it up and simply going to get a job elsewhere and never doing anything else to expose the wrong.
Edna's Law will eliminate this type of discloser.

The Bandwagon Discloser
For Whistle-blowers the good journalist is the only competent authority left. Journalists will often know who the genuine Whistle-blowers were in a case and it is vital that sources are never revealed.

A Bandwagon Discloser is someone who has not blown the whistle at all but when a scandal is exposed subsequently comes forward to the media. These are people who try to hog the limelight by alleging they are a Whistle-blower from a case.

They can appear in cases where there is an unnamed genuine Whistle-blower, who took all the risks to raise the concerns.

The Bounty Hunter.

If you require a financial incentive to disclose information, it is not whistleblowing because the motive is not public interest but self-interest.

Chapter Five
What Is The Public Interest?

I define the essence of "the public interest" in this section because there is as much ignorance on public interest as there is on the word Whistle-blower.

When you combine whistle-blowing and acting in the public interest, incredibly this is an area that the law has got so completely wrong, a fact that goes to the heart of PIDA, which is that PIDA includes everything that could be remotely argued to be public interest. This has resulted in protecting cases which are not public interest whistle-blowing at all.

If PIDA were viewed as a bottle containing doses of justice, there would be none left for the genuine whistle-blowers as it would have been used up on the trivial, misconceived and spurious claims considered whistle-blowing by PIDA. The public interest element in whistle-blowing has only been defined once by the courts, and then incorrectly defined (see below case) which is another fact that demonstrates the inadequacies and incompetence of PIDA and employment tribunals.

Edna's Law clearly defines public interest Whistle-blowing and whilst I am a care worker and not a lawyer, I can with total confidence state that the judge's reasoning in the below case is wrong and they have made a fundamental error in their defining judgment. Such an error would not occur in Edna's Law.

Chesterton Global v Nurmohamed (PIDA case)
This ruling is completely wrong because it completely fails to grasp the concept of what I know to be the only reliable measure in defining the public interest. That measure is motive.

Example A. If a worker reports that a company's accounts are being distorted, he is acting in the public interest because the act of distorting those accounts is wrong in itself. Whether or not the wrong-doing affects him or not, his primary motive for reporting the act of distorting the accounts is what would be tested under Edna's Law as it is the public interest element.

Example B. But if a worker reports that he is not receiving the correct salary because the company is distorting the accounts, this is not acting in the public interest, even if it is later argued in court that the issue affects a hundred other staff and claims the worker is acting in the public interest. The judge has incorrectly defined the concept of acting in the public interest by failing to grasp the motive demonstrated in Example B to define public interest.

Edna's Law is clear on this point: grievances about pay or bonuses are excluded from protection because the very nature of the issue is seeded in self-interest and wide open to misuse. It is reasonable to assume that if a worker is concerned about the rate of pay, he receives, no matter who else it affects, the original catalyst for raising the issue must be self-interest, therefore pay and bonus disputes are employment grievances and must be dealt with as such.

The two examples below are the only pay- or bonus-related issues that Edna's Law would protect:

If a Whistle-blower suffers a wage-related detriment as a result of whistle-blowing this is of course recognised.

If a Whistle-blower makes a disclosure that has nothing to do with his own wages but for example discovers his employer is paying slave wages to those working in a factory, this would be protected as whistle-blowing.

The public interest element should never be something that is put forward in a subsequent legal case in order to make the circumstances fit with the law.

The public interest element has to be there from the start, at the time of the act of disclosing, that it is the defining motive for acting in the public interest.

I therefore totally challenge the core reasoning of the judgment in the above case because doing a head count of who else may have been affected after the original alleged whistle-blowing, completely fails to capture the essence of public interest.

In this section I will define that essence.

I can instantly recognise the element of public interest because I know what it is that motivated me as a whistle-blower, I witnessed things that were so wrong I had to act and would do the same again without hesitation. Eighteen years' experience on a help-line has taught me how to recognise the essence of public interest in others and describe it clearly in words.

You will often hear public interest being applied to many different situations; it is something that can also be mis-used, for example being used as defence to justify something that is as far as it is possible to get from public interest.

For example, the police and/or the CPS are aware of evidence that would completely exonerate a suspect, they will justify that it is not in the public interest to disclose this information as it would jeopardize their case. To send an innocent person to prison in error is one thing but to deliberately withhold information that would exonerate an innocent person contravenes the rule of law and is most definitely not in the public interest.

In fact, the only prosecution that should take place here is one for Misconduct In Public Office - because that would definitely be in the public interest.

Many things are done allegedly in the name of the public interest, not all them right. I would guarantee that if the public were asked to vote yes or no to the following question "Is it in your interest to send an innocent man to prison?" the answer would be a resounding "no", as well as achieving a record turnout to vote.

I would consider the following examples as defining motives behind the genuine public interest motives. But as I said earlier the Whistle-blower acting in the public interest is not doing so as part of their employment role, the Whistle-blower acts outside their employment role in whistle-blowing and that is why they risk so much.

The Journalist: The defining motive of acting in the public interest, when disclosing information, is that the public have the right to know.

The Whistle-blower: The defining motive of acting in the public interest, is to stop the wrong-doing that is happening or is likely to happen to others.

Edna's Law would not allow any disclosure that was made for financial gain.

This can apply also to cases where an employee may have suffered a harm or may have discovered a risk as a result of a "near miss" incident he was involved in but the motive for disclosing the information is the risk to others.

There is no "me, mine or I" in Whistle-blower, there is only "you, others, and the public".

Example C. A worker hurts his arm on equipment at work and goes straight to a lawyer and sues. Regardless of what the lawyer might argue in court months later, this is not whistle-blowing because the worker made no effort to raise any concerns that others were at risk prior to going to a lawyer.

The lawyer is certainly not acting in the public interest by putting forward such a case, because every time someone who is not a Whistle-blower is protected by the law it adds to the injustice suffered by genuine Whistle-blowers who could not access that law at all.

Example D. A worker hurts his hand on equipment at work and immediately asks his employer to make safe the equipment because he is concerned that others are at risk. This is whistle-blowing. If the worker is forced from his job for disclosing this information and later needs a lawyer to bring a whistle-blowing case, it does not change the fact that the disclosure was made from a motive of public interest, concern for others at the time of disclosing.

These are the defining principles in recognising public interest acts under Edna's Law, which are to be used as the measure.

Again, I emphasise that no innocent employer has anything to fear from Edna's Law as it will protect them against the spurious claims of being a Whistle-blower that PIDA has been so effective at endorsing.

My Definition of the Essence of Public Interest Whistle-blowing
There is no Me, Mine or I in Whistle-blowing

In this section we will compare real cases:
The genuine Whistle-blower who will be protected by Edna's Law as opposed to The PIDA-protected self-interest discloser
I set myself the task of choosing just one case to demonstrate the core essence of public interest in

whistleblowing. I chose to challenge myself by looking at a very different sector to my own working background, a sector about which I knew nothing, so I chose the film industry.

In effect I put myself in a PIDA judge's shoes to see how difficult it would be to identify this essence (which has routinely escaped the judges in PIDA cases) from the available evidence. Despite an extensive search, I could not find any Whistle-blowers in this sector until I went back to 1937 and discovered Patricia Douglas – and I am so glad I did because the core essence of public interest screamed out at me from the pages of history when I read of her case. Patricia's is a case which would be protected under Edna's Law because she is a genuine Whistle-blower who meets all the criteria of our definition of acting in the public interest - even in the most traumatic of circumstances.

I must stress that those witnesses who came forward in the #MeToo movement are NOT whistle-blowers but witnesses whom I have every sympathy for, but the use of the term "**Speaking Truth To Power**" should never be used lightly.

Patricia Douglas IS a whistle-blower, you may wonder why you have never heard of her, because she is not a famous actress because she IS a whistle-blower.

These events happened in Hollywood in 1937.

Patricia Douglas was seventeen years old and she worked for the Roach Agency. She responded to a legitimate casting call from MGM studios via her agency and applied for the work. One hundred and twenty film extras were selected from all those who applied, and Patricia was one of them.

The girls were all told to report to the wardrobe department where they were dressed in skimpy cowgirl outfits and then were bussed out to a remote location that they believed was the film set.

When they arrived at the location, they discovered no film crews but waited there. Later that same evening two hundred and eighty-two MGM film salesmen arrived for a party and assumed that the scantily clad girls were there for their pleasure and the girls had no way to escape.

Patricia, who was teetotal, was held down by several men and had alcohol poured down her throat. She staggered to the bathroom and was sick and then went outside for air. One of the salesmen David Ross (who had a history of violence against women) attacked Patricia from behind and dragged her to a car where he brutally beat and raped her. A witness said later he saw her trying to fight off her attacker but subsequently retracted his statement.

Patricia was so badly beaten that she could barely see. She immediately reported the attack to the police and was driven to hospital by a police officer, who was later shown to have made no crime report. On arrival at the hospital Patricia was given a cold-water douche which destroyed any evidence and on arriving home she collapsed for fourteen hours. She then went to the Roach Agency and reported what had happened saying

"You ought to know what happened to me, so it doesn't happen to anyone else."

It was an accepted fact at the time that in such circumstances the victim would be offered a film contract, and everything would be hushed up, but Patricia did not want that. Instead she decided to fight back and said *"I was not trying to get anything. I just wanted someone to believe me."*

No woman in the history of Hollywood had ever even tried to link a sexual assault to a Hollywood studio. When failed by the law and by her employers Patricia took a landmark private prosecution.

When the District Attorney had not got back to her she hired a lawyer who issued the ultimatum that she would take the disclosures to the press.

The District Attorney, Burin Pitts, had been elected for a third term in spite of an indictment for perjury against him for another rape case involving a sixteen-year-old girl.

The District Attorney's election campaign was funded mainly from contributions from his close personal friend, Louis B Mayer, head of MGM studios.

Patricia said later that she *"knew she would be blackballed but she did not care, she wanted to be vindicated, to hear someone say you can't do that to a woman."*

The media ran the story front page naming Patricia and giving her address, they did not name MGM.

There followed an unparalleled smear campaign against Patricia with statements released alleging that she was a drunk and had venereal disease. Pinkerton detectives were hired to follow her and dig for dirt, but Pinkertons returned with a truthful report that indeed Patricia was teetotal and had been a virgin when raped.

Another of Patricia's witnesses was bought off by MGM and later documents revealed the extent of MGM's collusion and efforts to supress the truth.

When the law failed her again, she filed a further case, she left no stone unturned. In the end she was betrayed by her own lawyer and mother who was able to over-ride her wishes as legally she was a minor.

The District Attorney's case was reported at the time to have failed for the want of a prosecution, as the DA failed repeatedly even to attend the court to prosecute so the case was dismissed.

The experience haunted Patricia for the rest of her life. Her story was completely unknown until the film maker David Stenne came across her story whilst researching Hollywood and subsequently made a film about her called Girl 27.

Patricia Douglas was an extraordinarily brave young woman who was a genuine Whistle-blower.

Patricia reported events because she recognised that what happened to her could happen to others.

What Makes Patricia a Public interest Whistle-blower?
After reporting the events to the police, then collapsing for fourteen hours she went straight to her employer and her first words were:

"*You ought to know what happened to me, so it doesn't happen to anyone else.*"

In that one short sentence what Patricia demonstrated was that her motive in reporting her attack was to protect others from a similar fate. She was one of many girls that night that could have been attacked.

The circumstances that placed her to be in that situation were circumstances involving a real risk to others and whilst the danger to herself had passed, she was highlighting concern about the risk to others

She could not be bought off by a film contract, which was the accepted way of dealing with allegations at the time.

Patricia was failed by her employers, the police, the law but she still fought on, this is a trait of all genuine Whistle-blowers - they want the wrong-doing rectified and they never walk away.

I admire Patricia because she suffered a dreadful ordeal at a very young age and yet still her first thoughts were for the safety of others.

Hollywood and its treatment of women is of course a big debate opened up by the Harvey Weinstein case. I have sympathy for those victims.

But Patricia stands apart for me because she was a victim for a few hours, but she then became a Whistle-blower because she attempted to protect others and did so knowing full well that it would cost her a career.

Here are Patricia's words on why she fought through the courts:

"*I knew they would blackball me, but I wanted to hear someone say, you can't do that to a woman.*"

Patricia knew she would sacrifice her career in speaking out and did so anyway, at a time when the big studios really ran the whole of Hollywood. **That is speaking truth to power**. Never use the word Whistle-blower or speaking truth to power lightly.

I also note the words "*you can't do that to a woman*". She could have said "You can't do that to me" but there is **no ME** in Whistle-blower and Patricia Douglas was a Whistle-blower.

At a time when society values fame and celebrity so highly, how perverse that Patricia Douglas is not remembered because she was **no**t famous and the reason, she was not famous was exactly because she blew the whistle.

Know true courage when you see it.

Now let's look at another case to see how PIDA operates:
Ms Alrajjal v Media 10
Heard at: East London Hearing Centre   On: 24-26 January &
17 March 2017
Before:Employment Judge Ferris   Members: Mrs P Alford
Mr T Burrows

Representation
Claimant: Mr J Neckles (Trade Union Officer)
Respondent: Mr B Large (Counsel)
The unanimous judgment of the Employment Tribunal is that: -
The claim for direct sex discrimination, sex harassment and victimisation succeed;
The Tribunal awards the Claimant £6,500 injury to feelings;
The Tribunal also awards loss of earnings at £384.93 per week for 13 weeks from 1 November 2015 which is £5,004.09 together with an uplift pursuant to 207A Trade Union and Labour Relations Act of 10% which is £500.40.
The total award is £11,504.09

The Claimant is claiming direct sex discrimination, sex harassment and suffering a detriment for making a protected interest disclosure contrary to section 43B(1)(d) of the Employment Rights Act 1996 and victimisation.
The issues are listed comprehensively in the Preliminary Hearing Summary made by Employment Judge Hallen following the preliminary hearing on 14 October 2016.

The Tribunal heard evidence from the Claimant and for the Respondent from Mr Dale Nicholson, the Claimant's line manager, Haley Willmott who worked on the same sales team as the Claimant; Iain Large (no relation to the Respondent's Counsel) another member of the sales team; Emily Barton an HR Assistant; Mike Dynan one of the shareholding directors of the Respondent; Stephen Blackie who conducted a probationary appraisal of the Claimant; Johann Van Eeden a fellow probationer of the Claimant's; Mrs Jane Musgrove Human Resources Director. The Tribunal makes the following findings of fact.

In this claim for discrimination and whistle-blowing we are tasked with deciding first of all the issue of liability. We have been persuaded the Claimant was exhorted by Dale Nicholson to use her female allures so as to improve her sales performance. It is in that context that we find Dale Nicholson probably did say something to the effect of "wear a low-cut top" and did so by way of allusion rather than direct command. Dale Nicholson was not speaking as some sort of sexual predator but rather as an enthusiastic young manager of a sales team measured on performance.

We find that this was unwarranted conduct related to a relevant protected characteristic which had the effect, though not the purpose, of violating the Claimant's dignity or creating a humiliating or offensive environment for the Claimant. Dale Nicholson would not have used this method of improving sales performance among male team members and so there was also direct sex discrimination.

As to the allegation that Dale Nicholson instructed or insisted that the Claimant come to work when ill we do not so find. Dale Nicholson assertively tested how ill the Claimant was, but it was clear he would have done and did do the same for male employees who were claiming to be ill.

On 5 August 2015, the Claimant complained about the suggestion that she should use her womanly allures to improve sales. That complaint made a bit of a splash and email trails show that senior management were made aware. On balance the Claimant may have followed that oral complaint with what she intended to be a written grievance but through her ineptitude the written complaint was never communicated – it got lost, it was never chased, and the Claimant did not keep a copy.

The Respondent did not arrange a formal grievance following the oral complaint because on 7 August the Claimant wrote a conciliatory email which allowed the Respondent to put the matter to one side.

The Claimant was a probationer for three months. There was no elaborate written probation policy. But the expectation was for a fair and open assessment of the Claimant's skills and performance and a just outcome of a comparative assessment of the probationer members of the sales team.

The Claimant's assessment as a probationer appears to have been delayed and
She was dismissed on 1 October 2015. One other male colleague – Johann – was not dismissed but moved to an easier sales role. And the third probationer, Seb, was also dismissed. On the face of it the Claimant was the best of a bad bunch – none of them were anywhere near the rather optimistic sales targets selected for them. The Claimant was obviously the best in terms of sales achieved – surely the bottom line in a sales team.
The Claimant points to the juxtaposition of her relatively strong sales figures, and the discrimination – her clear oral complaints which produced a startled and concerned response in early August, and the Claimant makes the obvious connection. The Claimant contends that she was chosen for dismissal because she had complained about discrimination or at least that complaint was an important factor in the decision to dismiss. In our judgment a prima facie case has been made out for victimisation following the protected act, her oral complaint.

The evidence from the Respondent as to the appraisal of probationers and selection for dismissal suggested a shambolic process. This is an employer with over 250 staff but the Human Resources Director – a stakeholder in the Respondent – has no professional qualifications and none of the Respondent's participants have ever had any training in how to discipline and no equality training. The written process was discretionary for those without qualifying service. There was no engagement of any written process. There is no preliminary paperwork, no attempt to prepare relevant comparative information or preliminary reports from line managers. The appraisal process for the three probationers appears to have involved some of but not always the same managers. The managers took no notes. Their oral evidence as to what happened was confused and confusing.

If as seems probable Mike Dynan was the decision-maker, he responded to anecdotal reports from Dale Nicholson, the person complained about, and did not see any of the objective facts, except perhaps the raw sales information.

The Respondent had access to comparative phone records and digitally recorded arrival times as well as sales figures. Such information which could have been used in a fair evidence-based assessment was ignored apparently. On examination the phone records appear to show that the Claimant was more diligent as well as more effective than Johann, her comparator.

The Respondent insisted the Claimant was always late but there is no evidence of documented warnings, and the raw data would have been available to the Respondent but was never collated, still less examined comparatively. So we are left with an undocumented decision to dismiss with no rigorous process and in which major anecdotal unrecorded input came from Dale Nicholson, the subject of the sexual harassment complaint, and the decision-maker Mike Dynan had full knowledge of the allegation made against Dale Nicholson, but did nothing to procure an objective analysis based on something other than Dale Nicholson's perception of attitudes and potential.

The Respondent fails to persuade us that the decision was not made because of the previous sex harassment complaint against a key manager. The reverse burden of proof applies. We find not only that there was sex harassment and sex discrimination
Arising from the "womanly allure" incident but that the dismissal was an act of victimisation. The Claimant succeeds in her case that there was a dismissal in which the sex harassment complaint was an important trigger event in the decision to terminate her career with the company. We find that the Claimant's protected act – her oral complaint of sex harassment – was an important factor in the decision to dismiss. The Claimant's other complaints are dismissed.

The above judgment was given orally at the end of the liability hearing on 26 January. There was then a break during which there was an opportunity for the parties to disclose documentation and exchange witness statements relevant to mitigation. The Tribunal reminds itself in relation to the key issue of consequential loss, loss of earnings, that although the Claimant owes a duty to take reasonable steps *to mitigate her loss, the evidential burden to show that the Claimant has failed to mitigate her loss lies with the Respondent.*

At the remedy hearing we heard evidence from the Claimant and from Ms Musgrove. We make the following findings of fact.

The Claimant told us that she had not been able to find any alternative employment until nearly 12 months after her dismissal and then only part-time working in a supermarket. We note that the latest position appears to be that the Claimant is now fully mitigating her loss.

During the course of the Claimant's evidence the Claimant asserted that she had lived on benefits for an extended period of time after her dismissal. We regret to say that we do not believe the Claimant's evidence on mitigation.

The Claimant contended that her monthly rent was £1,100 for her studio flat in the City of Westminster and that the £1,100 included all her utility bills and council tax. The Claimant contended that she paid this monthly inclusive rent in cash. Unfortunately, the only bank account statements disclosed by the Claimant do not support that account. The Claimant contended that the Universal Credit payment made to her on an approximately monthly basis was used by her to finance the flat. First of all, that would not have left her with any income to feed herself or clothe herself or to travel around London. Secondly, the bank statements simply did not show the extraction of cash in total amounts during the course of a month to enable her (even in several tranches of cash) to have sufficient cash to pay the monthly rent.

Moreover, if one looks at the Claimant's credit card accounts, she is clearly a fairly free spender. During the course of the relevant period the Claimant spent over £700 on car insurance and was spending £30 or so in petrol every month as well as making purchases at bars and restaurants, cinemas, nail bars and so on. The Tribunal's difficulty with the Claimant's evidence is not limited to shortcomings in her evidence about her finances. The

Claimant demonstrated during her conduct of this case, by her language, her intelligence, her articulacy, that she was a highly motivated intelligent and resourceful individual. Nevertheless, in the 12 months following her dismissal it was the Claimant's case that the only work she could procure was part-time as a sales assistant in a local supermarket.

The Claimant has a University Degree and speaks fluent English and Arabic.
The Claimant has been immaculately turned out on every day of the hearing.

The Tribunal heard evidence called by the Respondent of the availability of work in media and in sales in London. The Claimant of course lives in Central London. The Respondent's case was that anyone with the Claimant's talents would have found work very quickly if they had needed to find work. The Respondent's case is that the evidence demonstrates that the Claimant is living a subsidised lifestyle. The Claimant herself admitted that a holiday in Venice had been paid by a friend. There is no evidence whatsoever in the financial statements disclosed by the Claimant for any holiday in Venice at the material time. It would appear that the generosity of her friend did not just pay for the cost of a holiday but paid for every ice cream, coffee, and meal.

In short it was apparent to the Tribunal that the Claimant had been less than frank about her financial circumstances and indeed about the seriousness of her attempts to find alternative employment. It was noteworthy that the Claimant had failed to produce any evidence of finding alternative employment before about August 2016, nearly 12 months after her dismissal. Such evidence as was produced was limited to a diary record based on the Claimant's own input maintained by the local job centre and a requirement of the continuing payment of benefits to the Claimant.

When a claimant fails to tell the truth about her circumstances post dismissal it is difficult for the Tribunal to form a reliable view of the facts in terms of the Claimant's claim for loss of earnings. The Claimant has succeeded on *liability, and she should not have been dismissed. Had there been a proper process she might have been provided perhaps should have been provided with an alternative opportunity in sales, instead of the comparator Johann. This was not a possibility which was investigated in the evidence examined by either the Claimant or the Respondent's representatives.*

Notwithstanding this shortcoming in the way in which the parties' respective cases were presented the Tribunal is satisfied that someone of the Claimant's calibre with good experience as a salesperson could have found equivalent alternative employment within four months of her dismissal. In other words, starting on 1 October 2015, the date for dismissal, an actively engaged claimant with the experience and intellectual resource of the Claimant could have found in the Central London area to which she had ready access from her astonishingly cheap residential accommodation, alternative employment commensurate with the employment at the Respondent. Accordingly, the Tribunal awards 13 weeks of loss of earnings (starting on 1 November 2015 and ending at the end of January 2016). The start date takes into account the one month's pay in lieu of notice which was given to the Claimant on her dismissal.

The Respondent by concession acknowledges that the entitlement to an uplift applies in principle in an "Equality Act dismissal" case. The Respondent contends that no relevant code of practice applies. The Tribunal respectfully disagrees. In this case taking a broad view of the evidence and exercising its function as an industrial jury the Tribunal concludes that an uplift of 10% is appropriate. The Tribunal has not found that the Claimant was the victim of a vindictive strategy. The Respondent was clumsy and incompetent and, in its failure, to observe appropriate processes it has been unable to demonstrate that it did not victimise the Claimant.

One of the parties' failures in the presentation of this case was the failure to investigate in the evidence the quantity and quality of benefits received by the Claimant during the material period of loss of earnings. Both parties were at a loss to address the Tribunal in closing submissions either on the facts of those benefits, or on the ways in which as a matter of principle any relevant benefits should be treated in connection with the loss of earnings award. In those circumstances the Tribunal has not sought to do the job of the parties' representatives and has made no deduction in respect of any benefits. This does not appear to be a case where recoupment applies because there is no evidence that job seeker's allowance was paid.

As to the claim for injury to feelings, this is a case where there were essentially two events – clumsy exhortation by Dale Nicholson to the Claimant to use her womanly charms in her capacity as an effective salesperson, and thereafter our finding dependent upon the reverse burden of proof that the dismissal was an act of victimisation. Acting as an industrial jury with collective longstanding experience of cases involving sexual harassment, we would put this particular example of sex harassment very low down on the tariff. The act of victimisation, involving a dismissal, has to be taken more seriously. Assessing injury to feelings necessarily requires us to consider the emotional impact of these events on the Claimant both in the short term and in the medium term. It was clear from the evidence given by the Claimant that she regarded the dismissal as irritating and unfair. Of course she was not the only member of this not very impressive probationary group of three to be dismissed, but the surviving member did not on the basis of the raw data available appear to be as good as the Claimant (though that is not saying much) and one can understand the Claimant's annoyance and disappointment with this treatment by the company following four months or so of her time and effort given to securing a permanent position as a member of the Respondent's sales team.

The Tribunal has had careful regard to the Respondent's extensive analysis of awards by other tribunals in not dissimilar cases. In the judgment of the Tribunal £6,500 is an appropriate award in this case. The Tribunal declines to make any award for aggravated damages. This was not a case where the Respondent behaved in an: "high-handed, malicious, insulting or oppressive manner in committing the act of discrimination".

Employment Judge Ferris 24 March 2017

My Response to Alrajjal v Media 10

This case would most certainly not be protected under Edna's Law because it is definitely not Whistle-blowing. Only PIDA and an Employment Tribunal could be so ignorant of genuine whistle-blowing as to reward someone in these circumstances whilst totally failing to protect thousands of genuine Whistle-blowers.

There is no public interest involved in the actions of Ms Alrajjal. It actually flies in the face of the rule of law. I leave the reader to decide on the facts.

Page 2 of the verdict infers that Ms Alrajjal intended to pursue this incident with a written grievance which the judge says may have been lost due to her ineptitude. On page 4 of the judgment it states Ms Alrajjal has a university degree. Every day I encounter genuine Whistle-blowers, all of whom have managed to make written accounts of the issues they care so much about, even those Whistle-blowers who have literacy or language barriers or visual impairments.

The verdict also states that two days after the alleged verbal complaint which is described as whistle-blowing, Ms Alrajjal does something I have never heard of a genuine Whistle-blower doing: she sends an email to her employer saying she does not wish to pursue the matter.

It is only when Ms Alrjjal's three months probationary period ends and she is not offered a permanent position that she resurrects the alleged earlier complaint and suddenly proclaims herself as a Whistle-blower.

I note that the Tribunal has completely failed to grasp that the employer has no motive to victimise Ms Alrajjal, after all she withdrew her earlier verbal complaint and did so in writing. Genuine Whistle-blowers are victimised for whistle-blowing: it is this act that makes them a threat to the employer.

There are some who would argue that reporting sexual harassment is whistle-blowing and yes, it is only if your primary motive in reporting it is concern for others, even if you are also affected. At no time in this case is there a hint of others or a hint of concern or any trace of impact.

Consider this: **a householder wakes up and discovers his house is being burgled and dials 999. Is this acting in the public interest at the time? No, of course it is not. It is the householder's self-interest that prompts the call.** I am not aware that anyone has ever dialled 999 in such a situation and said, "my house is being burgled but don't worry about me just make sure the burglar doesn't go into any other house on the street and burgle them when he has finished here." Apply this to the factual motive involved in Alrajjal.

The core public interest is clear to me and to all those who have spoken up genuinely in the public interest, but alas not clear to PIDA, employment tribunals or those described by the establishment as **"whistle-blowing experts"**, such as many academics, lawyers and those who benefit from promoting the compliance industry which surrounds the current system and PIDA - or as we genuine Whistle-blowers call it **"the whistleblowing gravy train"**.....all aboard, ignore the public interest and let's make some money of these people's misery!"

There were three probationers involved in the Alrajjal case; two were dismissed at the end of the three months and one was redeployed in another role.

The employer's paperwork and procedures are described by the Tribunal as "chaotic and shambolic" yet this chaotic and shambolic system is found to have been organised enough to target unfairly Ms Alrajjal (allegedly).

With regard to the word "harassment" used throughout this verdict my understanding of harassment is a sustained set of actions, not one single incident unless it is so serious that it causes fear of a repeat situation.

I do not class as harassment one comment made in bad judgment, that was the exception to the norm and was made by a very young and keen sales manager. It is not sustained; it has no impact on Ms Alrajjal or else she would firstly have complained in writing and secondly, she would not have withdrawn her grievance in writing.

Being aware of the levels of bullying, threats of violence, actual violence and sustained threats and verbal abuse that Whistle-blowers endure day after day, I would not consider the above incident as harassment at all, rather it was an ill-judged comment and nothing more. Harassment and victimisation are targeted and sustained acts, not one "off the cuff" comment. See Beyond the Façade and Breaking the Silence www.compassionincare.com for genuine examples of both harassment and hardship.

Edna's Law recognises harassment as a cumulative harm that builds to a level that breaks down the Whistle-blower's ability to take any more. It destroys heart and soul and trust. It is malicious and intentional.

The remainder of this verdict refers to Ms Alrajjal putting forward claims for consequential losses which are not backed up by evidence. The judge said *"We regret to say that we do not believe the claimant's evidence on mitigation. "When a claimant fails to tell the truth about her* circumstances post dismissal it is difficult for the Tribunal to *form a reliable view of the facts"* It is not difficult at all. Edna's Law will view lying for what it is.

Sadly, this case is among many I could have used. I have always made it clear that no innocent employer has anything to fear from Edna's Law, because only genuine Whistle-blowers are protected.

The next case **is not** public interest whistle-blowing

Robert Norman was a prison officer at Belmarsh Prison; he was also the union representative.

Robert Norman was jailed for twenty months for Misconduct in Public Office, after being paid for information by a journalist who worked at the Mirror Newspaper and later at The News of the World.

At the time of writing (June 2018), Mr Norman is taking a case to the European Court of Human Rights claiming that he was acting in the public interest.

Between 30th April 2006 and 1st May 2011, Robert Norman exchanged 40 pieces of information about Belmarsh Prison, for various sums of money totalling more than £10,000.

Mr Norman's barrister told BBC News South-East in January 2018 that *"there was nothing in the current law (PIDA) to say he could not receive payment for acting in the public interest"*

(Of course, I am well aware that there is nothing in PIDA to protect the genuine Whistle-blower and this case is just another example of how it is misused.)

I also note that the payments were paid into the bank account of Mr Norman's son, which indicates in my opinion a premeditated act to conceal the payments **and I would ask, why would someone take the action to conceal the payments if they truly believed at the time that they were acting in the public interest?**

Mr Norman's case raises the separate issue of a journalist or newspaper identifying a source, which should never have happened, and it breaks the first rule of journalism.

Please note the current law's failings include the fundamental failure to define public interest. Edna's Law would not protect or recognise any individual as a Whistle-blower who was motivated by the personal financial gain from disclosing the information.

Please note Edna's Law would not deter any Whistle-blower from speaking to the media as long as **no payment** was involved. I myself as a Whistle-blower have gone to the media and the facts were as follows:

The BUPA 7 case went part heard twice under PIDA, resulting in three hearings in all with many months in between. At the first hearing only my witness statement had been read and was in the public domain. I had been cross-examined for two days when the time ran out and the case went part heard.

Meanwhile we were fully aware at this point that one of the worst power abusers "MK" on whom we had blown the whistle was working in other BUPA homes on the orders of **BUPA director Des Kelly (now OBE), who is currently a trustee of the Relatives and Residents Association**. Even though Bromley Social Services had stated that MK should not work with vulnerable people, BUPA and Des Kelly completely disregarded this.

We knew that MK would continue to abuse vulnerable people as we had seen the extent of torture which she inflicted for pleasure. We decided to take my statement to the Express newspaper which ran the story:

"*Government advisor at centre of BUPA care home abuse*"

When we returned to the employment tribunal hearing some months later, I was cross-examined for a further two days opening with the accusation: "You sold your story to the Express didn't you?"

My response:" I would never take money for my story and I can prove it, I went to the Express to get Maria Keenahan named so she could be stopped from harming any more defenceless people and, if you had seen her do what I have, you would have done the same. Take money? I would have paid the Express to print the story and would do exactly the same again without hesitation."

The allegation was withdrawn of course because I could prove I was not paid, and the Express were willing to give evidence that no money was involved. The actual concept of being paid was abhorrent to me and is abhorrent to every genuine Whistle-blower.

There are some organisations e.g. WBUK and individuals who advocate financial incentives for Whistle-blowers. Yet as I have clearly shown this is directly at odds with the essence of public interest.

The Dodd Franks Act in the USA allows for people to claim a percentage of the funds in exchange for information, lawyers representing this type of "bounty hunter discloser", or who have gained information can also make a claim.

This is not whistle-blowing, but bounty hunting.
Anyone who could advocate financial incentives is as completely ignorant of the genuine Whistle-blower as it is possible to be. In fact, those who advocate this measure are actually harming genuine Whistle-blowers by lobbying for this perverse and anti-public interest measure. It paints genuine Whistle-blowers as money-grabbing bounty hunters out for themselves.

PIDA came into force in 1998. In that time, nothing has changed for the better and nothing ever will change until we replace PIDA with Edna's Law.

Edna's Law defines the essence of public interest whistle-blowing with the case of Patricia Douglas.

Eileen Chubb

Chapter Six
Why the EU Whistleblowing Law Will Fail

EU Whistle-blowing Law, page 1 paragraph 3
"Recommendation on protection of Whistle-blowers, setting out principles to guide States when introducing or reviewing rules for Whistle-blowers who report or disclose information on threats of harm to the public interest. These principles include essential components for effective and balanced rules that protect genuine Whistle-blowers whilst providing safeguards and remedies for those harmed by inaccurate or malicious reports"

My response: Whilst I fully agree that innocent employers should be protected from harm (and Edna's Law does more to ensure this than any other law), I do not agree with what is proposed by the EU in the above paragraph for the following reasons.

I note the words "*balanced rules*" in the same paragraph that is proposing that employers are specifically given

"Safeguards and remedies for those harmed by inaccurate or malicious reports"

My first reason is that genuine Whistle-blowers are those most at risk of being harmed by inaccurate or malicious reports and **no** remedy is being proposed for their protection which is hardly balanced.

Also, because the EU have encompassed an approach in all their recommendations that undermines any commitment to protecting Whistle-blowers. This is an approach mirrored by UK whistle- blowing law. I note the following content:

Appeasing employers by providing a remedy and safeguard that is not provided to Whistle-blowers equally should they be wrongly accused of making malicious allegations.

Stating in the body of the document that Whistle-blowers should respect their employer's right to a defence in how they put their case. **This is in effect giving employers the right to publicly smear Whistle-blowers as long as it is done in the name of a defence.**

No such statement is made to employers regarding respect for the Whistle-blowers.

The approach taken by the EU to win industry and business approval of the measures is mirrored by UK whistle-blowing law, PIDA, and an approach that places whistle-blowing law not under the Department for Justice, which is where it should be, but instead under the Department for Business, Energy and Industrial Strategy.

Unfortunately, such an approach has resulted in a weak and appeasing law that it has been wide open to abuse in its use against innocent employers.

Edna's Law ensures such remedies for employers are not needed in the first place because no harm has been done. Edna's Law is a strong law, written to ensure only genuine Whistle-blowers are protected, because if a law is to be effective it has already filtered out those who would use it for malicious reasons long before it reaches a court. Edna's Law has no need to appease or win support from the business sector before being implemented any more than the law on murder needs to win support from those who have committed no crime.

EU Recommendation Page 2 Paragraph 3
"According to the 2017 special Eurobarometer on corruption, around one in three of all Europeans (29%) think people may not report corruption because there is no protection for those reporting it. In the Commission's 2017 public consultation, fear of legal and financial consequences was the reason most widely cited why workers do not report wrong-doing"

I agree that there is fear of legal consequences of course because in the UK the legal consequence for the Whistle-blower is having to rely on PIDA.

There is predominant reference throughout the EU recommendations that protecting Whistle-blowers specifically from the financial sector would be especially beneficial for the EU.

Edna's Law protects all Whistle-blowers equally regardless of whether the issues relate to risk to life or fraud. Edna's Law does not discriminate against any genuine Whistle-blower because that would not comply with the concepts of rule of law, which requires that all are equal before the law. When you take the approach that has been thus taken on whistle-blowing, it effectively amounts to your whistle-blowing benefits me so I will protect you, whilst actively discriminating against Whistle-blowers from other sectors whose message is inconvenient or of no value to the State. Such an approach is in itself anti-public interest which is perverse for a public interest law. In Beyond the Façade, I state that there are two kinds of whistle-blowing:

The convenient
The inconvenient

Why does the State rush to protect one Whistle-blower and not the other? Edna's Law protects all Whistle-blowers equally regardless of what sector they come from. Consider this point especially when it applies to whistle-blowing law, **the essence of public interest has entirely escaped the law-makers of this planet**.

I believe in the rule of law and taking those principles and looking at where law works best, it is when those principles are incorporated. When they are not then you have a situation where the law and justice are two very different things and the result is laws such as PIDA. There is a remedy however and it is not the EU whistle-blowing law, but Edna's Law.

The EU Recommendations Page 4, "Better protection of the EU financial interests. Providing for strong Whistle-blower protection beyond the protection already granted to EU staff can make it easier to detect, prevent, and deter fraud, corruption, malpractices and other illegal activities affecting the EU financial interests, thus strengthening the relevant enforcement system. This system is currently built around the work of national authorities and the European Anti-Fraud Office (OLAF). It will in future be boosted by the European Prosecutor's Office (EPPO) Which will investigate and prosecute crimes affecting the EU budget"

My response:
There will be some who think we are daft enough to believe that this protection of money will help everyone BUT
Would it have saved Edna from torture? No
Would it have stopped her tormentors going on to torture others? No
Would it have resulted in the prosecution of both those responsible and those who covered it up? No

When those who hold those views can answer yes to all of the above then some credence can be given to their stance, but not before.

Edna is the measure for Whistle-blower protection.

EU recommendations page 4 paragraph 7 "The minimum standards in the proposed Directive aim for consistently high Whistle-blower protection across the EU, they aim to ensure Potential Whistle-blowers have clear reporting channels available to report both internally (inside the organisation) and externally (an outside authority)
When such channels are not available or cannot reasonably be expected to work properly, potential Whistle-blowers can resort to public disclosure
Competent Authorities are obliged to follow up diligently on reports received and give back to Whistle-blowers
Retaliation in its various forms is prohibited and punished

"If Whistle-blowers do suffer retaliation, they have easily accessible advice free of charge, they have adequate remedies at their disposal e.g. interim relief remedies to halt on-going retaliation such as workplace harassment or to prevent dismissal pending, the resolution of potentially protracted legal proceedings, reversal of the burden of proof"

There is nothing new here, it is the usual half page of procedures that can only be described as naive, self-serving, discriminatory and completely useless.

. If you have been overcharged for a fridge then free advice may be of benefit but Whistle-blowers need free legal representation.

. Remedies to halt on-going retaliation amount to placing Whistle-blowers at risk. By the point they have suffered the retaliation it is too late even for the small minority that can access such a remedy

. The resolution of protracted legal proceedings - there is no resolution to be had in whistle-blowing cases, it is not an issue of dispute to be resolved. What this amounts to is to settle out of court, hush up the wrong-doing and no genuine Whistle-blower considers this a resolution - it is merely something a sub-standard law forces them to do.

In short exactly all of the alleged promises of protection made by PIDA, which all look good on paper, in reality turn out to be completely and utterly useless.
See Edna's Law the 13 Steps later in this book, in order to recognise the detail and method of real protection as opposed to the above.

The proposed EU protection also states that only *staff who work for organisations that employ 50 staff or more will need whistleblowing arrangements in place*. This is incredible and demonstrates both the extent of discrimination and the ignorance involved.

How many people were employed at 21 Market Street, Hyde? Under 10
Would any of these staff have been protected by the EU if they blew the whistle? No.
If 21 Market Street were a small private practice in any country in the EU would the public want those staff protected so they could whistle-blow? Yes
21 Market Street, Hyde was the practice of the mass murderer Dr Harold Shipman.
It is completely naive to assume that all employers are fair-minded and welcome whistle-blowing. The very worst organisations have a culture of denial and self-preservation at any cost. The EU intend to hand to such organisations another means to punish Whistle-blowers: sanctions for making malicious allegations.
Do the EU really believe that every genuine Whistle-blower is not accused of making malicious allegations?
At the point my whistle-blowing was proven true by the prescribed regulator, BUPA knew this and yet went to the High Court to get our case struck out on the grounds it was malicious. This is a multi-national company operating in the EU and across the globe. They would welcome such a tool as the EU proposes to give them.
In spite of all the evidence we had in our case it was not enough and if I had a shred of doubt that anything would have been enough, then that last doubt has been dispelled by seeing the recently disclosed documents that have come to light among boxes of evidence obtained by the journalist, Niels Ladefoged under Subject Access law. All this evidence

will be published in the near future so I will only refer to one of the documents at this point. This document shows that BUPA were aware that apart from the seven Whistle-blowers, and the prescribed regulator's evidence, that other staff and witnesses when interviewed reported over 200 incidents that corroborated the original whistle-blowing concerns. Yet we were and **still are** to this day accused of making malicious allegations by BUPA.

Finally, the biggest flaw of all, there are two words relied on by the EU and those two words are "Competent Authorities"

Chapter 7
IN-competent Authorities

Why any law that relies on regulators to investigate is complacent and ineffective.

In order to fully understand why the measures in Edna's Law will fully protect Whistle-blowers, I need to demonstrate why what is currently in place completely fails to do this. The current law has completely failed to ensure that whistleblowing disclosures are acted on. Any proposed law that relies on prescribed regulators will fail to be effective, a fact that will cost lives and allow suffering, abuse and other wrong-doing to continue unchecked.

Firstly, I start this section by paying tribute to the small percentage who worked/work in such authorities, who truly fight every day to do their job and protect people. I would pay particular tribute to those who sacrificed their careers by speaking out and refusing to cross the line between right and wrong, in a system and in a country that demands that people **do not** care.

Consider the following,

There is widespread abuse in a care home

A number of staff report concerns to the management of the care home.

When no action is taken the staff take their concerns to the prescribed regulator.

The prescribed regulator thoroughly investigates and upholds the concerns in an inquiry report listing all the evidence relied on.

Would this be enough to stop the abuse? No, it would not and that is why PIDA fails.

Why? the first PIDA Case, The BUPA 7,

7 whistle-blowers went to BUPA management reporting abuse and when no action was taken, they went to the PIDA prescribed regulator, who fully investigated and upheld the concerns. The BUPA response to this;

The 7 Whistle-blowers are liars
The prescribed regulator is a liar
The 30 other witnesses are liars
The independent pharmacist is a liar

The medication records are a lie

Further abuse scandals at this home continued to be reported in the press several years after the original whistle-blowing case.

In effect Mr Turner and his colleagues from the prescribed regulator upheld the abuse and then when they gave evidence on behalf the Whistle-blowers that the abuse and subsequent harassment was true, BUPA attacked them. The denial was to such a degree that even the prescribed regulator had to be became a Whistle-blower, they knew the evidence and held the line, **but it was not enough to stop the abuse, because the company were beyond the law.** To this day BUPA continue to deny the truth, my book *Beyond the Façade*, tells the full story, the book was published in 2008 and has never been challenged by BUPA because every word is true, and I can prove it is true with hard evidence.
So even when against all the odds a prescribed regulator or competent authority does everything right, it was not enough to save Edna or the other vulnerable people from further abuse.
Since the BUPA 7 case things have got progressively worse. What today's Whistle-blowers have to face are prescribed, allegedly competent authorities who are **anything but** competent and who do **not** act or investigate. The best that can be hoped for currently is *they do not tell your employer your name if you whistle-blow.

*CQC give 47 whistle-blower's names to employers

We now have authorities that are so dysfunctional, dishonest, complacent, self-serving and totally incompetent that the abuse and suffering of vulnerable people has reached epidemic proportions.
Whistle-blowers do not have authorities they can go to in order to report abuse, **instead they have authorities that aid and abet the abusers**

Incompetent Authorities: Safeguarding

Compassion in Care has gathered evidence on these
failures for years and all this evidence is available in full on
www.compassionincare.com see the following,
Tales of the Un-Inspected Over 300 reports from undercover
visits to care homes.
https://compassionincare.com/breakingthesilence Evidence
from Whistle-blowers and relatives.
Evidence on failures of regulators, safeguarding and other
authorities Reported weekly for two decades.
Whilst we have been continually exposing **the myth of
safeguarding**, other charities have been more than happy
to perpetuate this safeguarding myth whilst generating huge
amounts of income from selling safeguarding training to local
authorities, who have purchased this training with public
money. The lack of value for money of these authorities'
safeguarding standards is evidenced by scandal after
scandal of abject failures.

There are even some charities that have argued and
continue to do so that if the "safeguarding adults" process
was as robust as the safeguarding children's process then it
would stop abuse. **This is of course the same
safeguarding children process that is supposed to have
protected
The children of Rotherham
Rochdale
Oxford
Victoria Clambie
Baby P
Eli Cox**
And tragically, hundreds more.

I could choose from hundreds of reports to show beyond
doubt why the safeguarding process is
Incompetent
Dysfunctional
Fractured
Unqualified
Unlawful
Unsafe

Secret and therefore unaccountable.

Most of all it is processed by disengaged individuals who have distanced themselves from the suffering of humanity and if I had to sum them up in one sentence it would be, **"Let's get the abusers to investigate themselves but don't let anyone find out"** When the initial Safeguarding fails and if the families are able to shout loud enough for long enough, then Safeguarding will investigate themselves with an SAR which is a Safeguarding Adults Review. The aim of this whole process is to:
State what the previous failures to act were but be careful to do this in an environment (SAR) where no one will ever be held to account or any blame attached.

Promise each family of the thousands failed by the original safeguarding non-inquiry that this time, lessons have been truly learned (and then do the same next time and the time after and so on).
Say you are truly sorry for what happened (look like you mean it) now you have been caught out.

Beech Lodge Care Home which belongs to Sussex Health Care, is just such a case. Three years after the first so-called Safeguarding panel failed to investigate how **two adults were admitted to hospital on the same day, both with broken femurs, both from Beech Lodge**. A Safeguarding Adults Review **re**-investigated the original Safeguarding investigation and as usual found serious failures. The re-investigation is the result of the families' continual fight for the truth.

This case is a home belonging to a company we first raised concerns about to the Department of Health in 2015 but we are still waiting for Jeremy Hunt and his successors to reply on these issues. Our reports, **CQC - An On-Going Concern** and **CQC, A Likely Story** can be found on the Compassion In Care website along with all the correspondence to the Health Department.

The below list shows those authorities who were involved with both victims at the time of the original investigation:

THE BEECH LODGE RE-INVESTIGATION REPORT

"The following agencies were identified as being involved with both Matthew and Gary"
. *Sussex Healthcare*
. *Sussex Police*
. *West Sussex learning disabilities contract team*
. *Care Quality Commission*
. *West Sussex adult services*
. *Surrey County Council*
. *London Borough of Camden*
. *Sussex Partnership NHS Foundation Trust*
. *Clinical Commissioning Group*
. *South East Coast Ambulance Service*

Those listed below were asked to review the original failures
"Each organisation produced an individual management review (IMR).

A Safeguarding Adult Review (SAR) panel was appointed to work with the reviewer with representation from the following agencies

. *West Sussex learning disability operations manager*
. *Care Quality Commission inspection manager*
. *Sussex Police detective chief inspector*
. *Horsham & Mid Sussex CCG head of quality and nursing*
. *Surrey and Sussex Healthcare NHS Trust*
. *Surrey County Council*
. *London Borough of Camden*
. *Safeguarding adult's board manager*
. *Sussex Partnership NHS Foundation Trust"*

The following are just a few extracts from the full report which can be found on our website
"The main questions they are seeking answers to are:
. *How did the injuries to their loved ones occur?*
. *Why did they occur?*
. *Who at a staff and corporate level is responsible?*
. *Has there been any collusion to hide the truth?*

In order to gain answers, they have, and will continue to, take their concerns to whatever level is required. This includes legal advice and the use of the local and national press. To that end, they have already made a number of complaints and informed the Ombudsman. They have also asked for and received documents from various agencies and had meetings with individuals in senior positions."

Matthew's parents explained that they accept that accidents occur, and if individual agencies or organisations had accepted that they had made a mistake and fully explained how it happened, they may have accepted it. However, they do not believe that the system has done that. On a simple point, they expressed disappointment that the care home provider never sent a card or acknowledged Matthew's plight in the days after the injury occurred.

Gary's brother stated that he now had a total distrust of the agencies. He stated that he expected agencies to safeguard his brother, but he believes from what he has witnessed, that they are only supporting the agencies who harmed him.

The author has worked with the families to explain the function of the Safeguarding Adults Review. He has also made them aware that the review may not be able to obtain answers to all their questions, especially how the injuries occurred.

Whilst this review will examine the actions of various agencies, it is important to highlight how these injuries and the subsequent professionals' interaction with the families has impacted on the individuals. The author has spoken to Matthew's and Gary's family members on a number of occasions. He also visited Matthew and Gary, with the support of family members.

The families of both Matthew and Gary emphasised that both men had sustained a traumatic and very painful event, and whilst both have settled down in new care homes, the families have explained that both Matthew and Gary are still suffering. Gary in particular, misses the friends that he made at Beech Lodge, both having been residents since 2003. They had to endure great pain and long stays in hospital.

Both families have expressed concerns about how agencies have responded to the injuries. Despite the high level of contact they have had with a number of the agencies, neither family are satisfied with the outcomes and are sceptical about how impactful the safeguarding adult review process will be in providing answers. One family member in particular has asked that "sceptical" be changed to no confidence.

"They believe that agencies have not been open and honest with them and have genuine concerns that they are potentially colluding to hide the truth from them. Their main concern has been the influence that they believe the care home providers have had on the process, and they have continually highlighted the fact that the West Sussex County Council cabinet member for adult services until recently was a director of The Care Home Company.

"Whilst this could have been a coincidence it is concerning as these injuries are unusual in immobile patients and these two patients have relatively thick bone cortex despite one having a diagnosis of osteoporosis. I do not think these fractures would have occurred spontaneously and DO have concerns that they may have been sustained as a result of a non-accidental injury"

This was an important entry that encapsulated the serious concerns of the Consultant and should have informed future action until further evidence became available.

The prompt identification of the safeguarding concerns by staff in the Emergency Department, which led to the consultation with the Trust safeguarding team and notification, was good practice and demonstrated the vigilance and awareness of staff to adult safeguarding issues.

A separate Safeguarding alert form (SVA1) was completed for each of the patients by different individuals. These were submitted to West Sussex Safeguarding Community Learning Disabilities team via the hospital based West Sussex social worker who emailed the alerts at 17:28.

Both forms lacked detailed information. There was no explanation of the safeguarding concerns, (section 2 on both forms) this section was left blank. On forms the question, are the police aware or involved? If yes give details, were marked "Yes" with no further details. It has now been established that the police had not been informed on the day by any agency and did not become aware until 9th of April 2015.

Observations
There were at that early stage a number of hypotheses as to how the
injuries to Gary and Matthew could have occurred, they ranged from,
. Complete accident
. Avoidable accident
. Deliberate act

The last two options could potentially have been criminal acts including assaults such as Section 20. Securing of evidence at an early stage was essential to establishing the facts.

The consultant recorded that their belief was that the injuries sustained by both individuals were potentially non-accidental. This indicates a possible deliberate act and therefore a crime. The police should have been the lead agency and should have been involved at an early stage

"The individual management review confirmed the following:
In addition, the Trust safeguarding policy does in fact state as a duty for the ward manager /matron:
"Discuss allegations with social services and ensure any other agencies have been informed or involved, e.g. police. If necessary, contact the police directly.

Breye Preston shoot (2017) report into learning from London SARs highlights the following
"The timing of information sharing was recognised as crucial too. One SAR emphasised the importance of early information sharing with police by agencies such as the ambulance service, adult social care and hospital, in order

not to miss forensic opportunities relating to a possible crime scene."

The explanation as to why the police were not informed by the hospital or why forms were not completed correctly appears to be one of communication failure between different teams leading to confusion.

Set out at section 3 within the hospital there is an in-house safeguarding team. It was this team that the consultant and emergency department staff liaised with, specifically the named nurse for safeguarding adults. The nurse believes that she contacted Surrey social services to inform them about Matthew and Gary.

MY RESPONSE. Too many people and too little action is the translation for all this jargon. Whenever I read the hundreds of reports just like this, I find myself wondering how much more I have to read before I get to the line about what actually happened, that line being that they left the care home/hospital to investigate themselves and they found themselves innocent.
If such a method of investigation was effective it would be used to save resources and demand on the court and prison budget, with all defendants simply asked to fill in a guilt self-assessment.

"Given the serious concerns that were recorded by the consultant, there is no clear explanation as to why the police were not contacted. It could be that having made a referral to West Sussex hospital adult social care team, it was believed that they would make the decision in respect of further action.
It may be as expressed by the safeguarding nurse, that they believe that social services from either Surrey or Sussex is not clear to which area team she spoke stated they would inform police. There is no clear record of any such decision being made.

19 of the twenty-seven SARS as identified learning about how practitioners record their work, or how the organisations provide them with recording systems and processes. The issues were diverse, but a common scene was an absence of key information in the case record.

On discussion with the staff nurse it appears that the family have expressed concerns and advice was given that if beach Lodge feel it relevant to find out what has happened then they can internally investigate but as far as safeguarding it has been logged as an incident "

MY RESPONSE. This is what safeguarding is, log it on a form, stick it in a drawer and forget about it. I note the above section states "That if Beech Lodge feel it relevant to find out what happened..." Two men people suffer horrific fractures to their femurs and the translation for how safeguarding viewed it is

If the home want to find out what happened they can, we can't be bothered it's been logged that's all we do"

"The failure of the system was highlighted in June 2015 police investigation. An individual thought to be the agency carer who left the room before Gary was hoisted, when interviewed by police denied being at the home. Beech Lodge staff were unable to identify him to confirm that he had been working. It is not clear if the individual interviewed was working and lied, or someone who was using his identity to work illegally in his place. This raises a number of concerns, why would he lie, and if he is not lying an unknown individual reporting to be someone else was working with vulnerable adults."

MY RESPONSE What I would have looked at is the timesheets submitted by the individual for the month and from that isolate the date that the incident took place; because both the care home and the individual would have a copy of this document and it can be cross- referenced. These records are required by law to be retained by the home for tax purposes.
If it were an agency worker then the agency needs to produce copies of all timesheets submitted by staff for that

period, which they are required to keep by the tax office. The names can then be cross-referenced to staff files.

The names of staff on the above records then need to be cross-referenced with the home's MAR sheets (medication records) and care plans which will show who was on duty that night.

Then interview the suspects and present them with the above evidence and ask them who would have hoisted Gary and Matthew in that time frame.

"It weren't me guv", might be the start of the suspects interview but it should not end the interview.

"There appears from an early stage of the enquiry, to have been an assumption that manual handling is the probable cause of the injuries to both individuals. At that time, there was no evidence other than feedback from the care home management that this was the cause of the injuries"

MY RESPONSE This is what is happening with safeguarding across the country. I have sat in on numerous safeguarding meetings to support families, it's painful to watch the process. It's like watching a snail carry a rock uphill. The complacency, ignorance and total lack of common sense is staggering and if this is what they can describe as a competent authority then the word competent needs to be changed in the dictionary. **In effect people need to be safeguarded from safeguarding.**

Example Two, Safeguarding Adults Review Mendip House Care Home:

"The company has registered 58 homes and Community Services across England, providing around 250 beds, almost a third of providers locations are within the South West. During May 2016 6% of the providers registered locations were outliers with high abuse notifications, higher than expected for the size and type of service....

The CQC acknowledges that events to which it was alerted during November 2014 and August 2015 should have triggered a discussion concerning a potential inspection....

MY RESPONSE, Triggered a discussion? The events they were alerted to are not included in any CQC inspection report nor are they disclosed anywhere in the SAR. When you look at the detail of those events that the authorities expected to merely "*trigger a discussion on the safeguarding scale of judging such things*" then you see the ingrained level of complacency that exists in these agencies.

We obtained the below information via a Freedom of Information (FOI) request:

In 2015 CQC were informed that the following incident has occurred:

A staff member made a person eat pizza covered in mustard followed by yoghurt with mustard in, the person was sick, the sick was then put into a glass of water which they were made to drink. **This information would trigger a very different response under Edna's Law.**

The regulator found 25 multiple breaches of the health and social care act 2008 regulated activities regulations 2014 once it was alerted to the poor oversight of practice at Somerset House.

MY RESPONSE The regulator CQC (which we will deal with in the next section), has one talent and that is to go into homes where people have died, been tortured, been abused or totally neglected - AFTER it has been exposed by either the media or Whistle-blowers. The Regulator will only then say, "Actually this home is not so good, it's pretty bad now you come to mention it." **That is not a regulator it's a reactor.**

"It beggars' belief that staff were asked to sign a declaration each time they had a formal supervision session to confirm they have not witnessed any abuse. Ditto evidence uncovered by the enquiry team in their reviews of previous safeguarding queries revealed that the provider had routinely conducted internal investigations into the poor or abusive conduct of the Rohn staff members in isolation and without reporting outcomes to either SCC or CQC.

MY RESPONSE, It does not surprise me at all. I would have asked why in numerous CQC inspection reports does it state that inspectors checked staff supervisions were taking place and records checked? Why did CQC not notice much earlier what the staff were being asked to sign? I note this practice and the negative impact on any Whistle-blower in relation to the EU malicious allegations remedy, where the signing of such a document would be used against the Whistle-blower.

"*Is recorded evidence that often a Whistle-blower would resign, whilst the alleged perpetrators were given warnings following disciplinary and retained or recycled within the home. The former is an astonishing practice which arguably played a key part in the duration of abuses at Somerset Court since the CQC enquiry team found that it was ineffective the latter may constitute wilful neglect the documentation does not evidence that provides understanding of the role of the responsible individual* "

MY RESPONSE See how many of those Whistle-blowers were able to access PIDA. I am unable to find any.

"*The circumstances of the whistleblowing concern in Mendip and elsewhere that employee deviance was harming residents (author's note: ABUSE in English), compromising the services and working conditions at Somerset Court as well as that the provider company it is unusual to have a full understanding of the Whistle-blowers intentions, the processes used by the hour and the consequences for those who are involved*"

MY RESPONSE With Edna's Law, there would be no such lack of understanding; this is exactly the type of case that would result in a prison sentence.

Please note that we have made specific recommendations to the Law Commission in relation to Misconduct In Public Office with specifically the intention that CQC should be prosecuted in such cases as this under MIPO. Should these recommendations subsequently not be acted on by the Law Commission then Edna's Law will incorporate this in a later report, whereby individuals at CQC will be liable for a prison term for such cases as this.

Be under no illusion: the extent of the suffering that is allowed to happen and allowed to continue to happen is the result of relying on safeguarding and CQC as competent authorities. Edna's Law would not treat their conclusions in any cases as credible evidence.

The few examples that I have given are not unique, they are typical. For years we have been exposing such failures and our work shows beyond any shadow of a doubt the truth of this.

Please see www.compassionincare.com for the following evidence

Breaking the Silence Part 1
Breaking the Silence Part 2
Breaking the Silence Part 3
Tales of the Un-Inspected
Safeguarding Shambles Parkview Parts 1 and 2
Safeguarding Shambles Morris care
Merok Park Care Home.
CQC An Ongoing Concern
CQC A Likely Story
CQC Contempt for Evidence
Evictions and Restrictions
The Jeremy Hunt letters
The Andrea Sutcliffe CQC letters
65 issues of *Private Eye* exposing CQC failures, commencing with the lies they told about closing 100 care homes exclusively exposed in a joint investigation by Compassion in Care and *Private Eye* magazine.

All our evidence is clear: the prescribed regulator CQC (for England) cannot be relied upon to:

Act on the wrongdoing

Protect the Whistle-blower's identity

Inform the public of all information known about a care home or hospital as the video of a CQC meeting shows, can they even recognise what a Whistle-blower is in the first place.

The Police and the Crown Prosecution Service (CPS)

Edna's Law has very clear recommendations for these two organisations (see relevant sections for full details). First, I would highlight the following issues in order to make clear what needs to be addressed.

The deliberate suppression of evidence as exposed by *The Sunday Times Tom Harper* in May 2018.

The failure to prosecute serious crimes is just a snapshot of a very real problem that has resulted from

A lack of resources

A lack of accountability for those who suffered a miscarriage of justice

The complete failure of the rule of law

Prosecutions based on an agenda and not on evidence

A complete waste of public money that could be put to better use in holding people to account that are actually guilty.

A complete lack of accountability for those in public office who have deliberately suppressed evidence or who have been incompetent or complacent in failing to obtain or disclose evidence known to exist.

Other examples are the numerous cases e.g. of rape suspects wrongly charged or prosecuted. The safeguarding process in relation to the police has also led to a situation developing where the most vulnerable are downgraded by the justice system:

Where the safeguarding process has impeded the police investigation where crimes against elderly people are rarely prosecuted at all where **everybody thinks somebody else should be dealing with it.**

 Coroners' Courts

This is yet another area we have many concerns about, especially in relation to evidence from Whistle-blowers which can be excluded as not relevant; also, in relation to evidence about a lack of care being excluded.

For example:

The evidence from a Whistle-blower in relation to the Crossrail death of **Rene Tzacik**.

Parkview Care Home in Bolton Parts 1 & 2 regarding evidence about a care home's practices and whether nursing checks were done post head injury, when no nurses were on duty.

Another recent case regarding the lack of care of a young person leading up to her death being considered irrelevant.

I would summarise the concerns' I have in relation to how coroner's courts deal with vital evidence as:

A man gets on the bus and is administered a slow acting poison, which is witnessed by another passenger. The man gets off the bus and gets on a train where he dies sometime later. The coroner does not want to hear about the evidence from the witness on the bus as the death occurred on the train.

Incompetent Authority Summary

Sometimes the existence of **too many** authorities can be a problem in itself especially when so many of these authorities are so incompetent. Most people believe the existence of such regulators is a good thing until the day comes when they have to use them. It is only then that the total lack of redress becomes painfully apparent.
Strangely enough the reaction to this problem demonstrates a lack of common sense.
I attended the Law Commission event on Misconduct In Public Office along with members of the public, Whistle-blowers and campaign groups, all of whom had first-hand experience of being completely failed by such authorities as CQC, Safeguarding and the Ombudsman. These failures exceeded the boundaries of incompetence and met the threshold for Misconduct in Public Office.
One person suggested the need for an authority to investigate the authorities that failed. However there would eventually be the need for yet another authority to investigate the authority that failed to investigate and so on until we **stop this waste of time and resources and deal with the true issue** and that is the real need for an effective and fair law that holds those responsible to account regardless of political or other agendas.
We as a society have never needed accountability more than we do today and have never achieved it less: Edna's Law is about bringing the law and justice together in the interest of all.
Finally I would like to deal with Jeremy Hunt's woeful parody of protecting Whistle-blowers in the NHS, the Robert Francis QC Inquiry, which I read on the day it was published (see Robert Francis Joke book on YouTube) and responded that it would not be long before the next hospital scandal had a health minister saying yet again we must do more to protect Whistle-blowers.

Jeremy Hunt said after Mid Staffs:
We need to do more to protect Whistle-blowers.

Jeremy Hunt said after Gosport:
We need to do more to protect Whistle-blowers.

I wonder how long before Mr Hunt says again "We need to do more" as he is currently hoping to be the next chair of the Health Select Committee, a position which would give him immeasurable scope to say "*we need to do more*". **Forever confessing the need to do more is evidence of how little has ever been done, the same mistakes playing over and over like a nightmarish version of groundhog day.**

In June 2018 *Private Eye* magazine reported (*Medicine Balls*) that Whistle-blowers are being asked to swear an oath that they have not disclosed to Private Eye. It seems that public interest disclosures should never be **disclosed**! Most of all to such a competent and effective authority as *Private Eye*, as it may result in public awareness, outrage and accountability.
The same issue of *Private Eye* has excellent coverage on the Gosport and the Belfast Dunmurry Manor scandals, which again highlighted the incompetent and negligent authorities involved in the failures.
I note that Northern Ireland in particular has used Des Kelly the individual who covered-up the BUPA 7 abuse for advice on social care (Des Kelly OBE) so it is hardly surprising what such advice harvests.
The Gosport War Memorial Hospital families have fought for years (as all those who have suffered grave injustices are forced to do in the UK) to get a degree of truth exposed. These families are now calling for criminal prosecution. They should not have to call for this - it should have been done long ago. **Those who abuse are those most protected by the law.**
I also note the *Sunday Times* 24/6/2018 and the Whistle-blower from inside the inquiry exposing the cover-up on syringe drivers that should have been included in the report. Alas even at this point of long fought for justice, there is still a cover-up involved.

One final point on Gosport: the inquiry states that hundreds of lives were "**shortened**", this terminology is in itself very telling - if 50 people were killed in a train crash the headline would not be **"50 people's lives shortened in train crash."** People's lives were **taken unlawfully** at Gosport War Memorial Hospital, not "*shortened*" **this word devalues the priceless worth of each life taken.**

I have exposed layer-by-layer and laid bare the uncomfortable and worrying reality of such authorities for years. Those who risk all to speak out deserve nothing less than Edna's Law.
Edna's Law defines the only competent authority as one which

Has the expertise and experience to investigate crime

That can be openly challenged by those who reported the crimes and who have the knowledge to question.

That all such challenges are published

Edna's Law recognises that **only** transparency begets competency

Chapter Eight
Examples of Edna's Law Qualifying Disclosures

Before I move on to some brief examples of disclosures, I want to include Edna's Law recommendations for Whistle-blowers who have signed the Official Secrets Act, these are the Whistle-blowers who risk the most. I submitted my recommendations to The Law Commission in response to their call for evidence. This is the most difficult area of whistle-blowing, so we tackled this first and submitted the below report to the Law Commission. It is worth reading this section in relation to the rule of law, because it will affect you personally if as a member of the public you object to for example, your Government going to war illegally.

No Whistle-blower from this sector has told me they expect to be protected by Edna's Law in the same way as Whistle-blowers from other sectors but wish to be able to defend themselves in a fair hearing and therefore Edna's Law asks for the following:

PUBLIC INTEREST – ENEMY No 1
Whistle-blowing and the Official Secrets Acts by
Eileen Chubb
©February 2017

Introduction

This report is in response to the law commission proposals on the official secrets act.
 Which amount to the **greatest attack on free speech** in generations. This consultation will directly affect Whistle-blowers and whilst accepting that the area of Official Secrets needs to balance safety and freedoms our concern is that freedoms are being taken away by stealth.

Firstly, we are concerned
That any Whistle-blower who is charged with a criminal offence under any **new** or existing legislation is given a **fair hearing** and the chance to defend themselves to the same degree as **any** other citizen charged with a criminal offence. That there is **no** increase in prison terms and

That any amendments made to this area of law are made to improve the law in the interests of fairness, transparency and justice, not for political motives.

Secondly, we completely reject the inclusion of **Damage to the Economy** as a new offence because this could be misused by the state to protect the corporate interests of private companies to the degree that any damaging information could be suppressed for fear of prosecution.

Thirdly it is essential that we have a free press who protect their sources and who must have access to a public interest defence in order to serve the public interest.

Whistle-blowing or Espionage?

As neither the current Law nor the recommendations for new legislation in the form of **The Protection of Official Data** make **any** clear distinction between **Espionage** and **whistle-blowing** and **other leaking**, we suggest the following categories:

Espionage: An individual who intentionally obtains information for the purposes of giving an advantage to either another state or a hostile entity with the intent of causing harm to the public or the state.

Whistle-blowing: An individual who during the course of their work is confronted by evidence of wrong-doing and who either

Discloses the evidence internally but no action is taken to address the wrong so then they would have to decide whether or not to go outside,

or the internal route is compromised or inadequate, resulting in disclosure to the public with **only** the intent of serving the public interest by stopping the wrong-doing.

Other Leaking: There is also the category of leaking for other reasons, political or financial gain or personal motives for example. This category needs to be clearly and separately defined because this is **not** whistle- blowing and should be a separate issue.

Clearer terminology should be used as "leaking" is too broad a term.

There should be a non-exhaustive list of examples of **what is** and **what is not** a Public Interest Disclosure. I suggest that a public consultation on this list should take place separately, making specific efforts to include whistle- blowers from all the sectors covered by the current Official Secrets Act, both from the UK and **also** from the countries whose legislation the Law Commission included in their consultation paper 230. There should be no new legislation without this important point being clarified. We are already working on gathering information from all sectors as part of our work on Edna's Law. We have the advantage of our many years of experience in being contacted by Whistle-blowers from all sectors, because this is the reality that underpins Edna's Law.

Burden of Proof
The Law Commission Consultation (Page 45)
*"As we discussed in our analysis of the current law, one of the aims of the Official Secrets Acts 1911 and 1920 was to **ease the prosecution's burden** in respect of proving elements of the offences in the Official Secrets Act 1911.*
*For example, section 1(2) of the Official Secrets Act 1911 provides that the prosecution does not need to show that the defendant committed any particular act tending to show a purpose prejudicial to the safety or interests of the state. Notwithstanding that no such act has been proved against them, **the defendant may be convicted** if, from the circumstances of the case, or from the defendant's conduct, or **from their known character as proved**, it appears that their purpose was a purpose prejudicial to the safety or interests of the state. Therefore, the prosecution does **not** need to prove beyond reasonable doubt that the defendant had a purpose prejudicial to the safety or interests of the state. It suffices that **it appears** the defendant had such a purpose **from their known character."***

With regard to "**easing the prosecution's burden**" if there is **no evidence** other than somebody's subjective opinion, **there should not be any prosecution**. As an organisation which is evidence-based, we find this particularly alarming and so should everyone, because most people are unaware that this is current law. The presumption of "**innocent until proven guilty**" is a fundamental right. **To place the burden of proof on the accused undermines the right to a fair hearing**.
For example, Mr X had a criminal conviction for burglary as a teenager and has never re-offended and is now a

hardworking family man who bitterly regrets the crime of his youth. Mr X is on his way home from work and is arrested as it "**appears because of his known character**" that he was intending to break into a house he passed by on his route home.

Private Companies

Damage to the Economy. The information given for this new inclusion is sufficient to raise serious concerns about the possible consequences. The term insofar as it affects the national interest could be applied to the corporate interests of any large organisation. **No corporate interest should be protected by the state. If there is damaging evidence about an organisation that affects the public then it is in the public interest for it to be disclosed**. For example, if a Whistle-blower disclosed documents about wrong-doing at a bank and the bank collapsed as a result, could this be twisted into "damage to the economy"? The fact such a possibility is being considered at all is chilling.

Attorney General
*Law commission Consultation page 74. 3.113 "The essence of the Attorney General's function under the Official Secrets Acts is that **he draws upon his political experience** and is able to obtain the views of the responsible minister on the national interests, for the purpose of exercising more efficiently his impartial law enforcement role. He is not influenced by party considerations in exercising this role"*

I consider this an **unsafe process** for impartial judgment because there is clearly a potential conflict of interest. For example, if a particular Minister or Government have been damaged by disclosures made by a Whistle-blower and the views of that same Minister are allowed then to directly influence the decision to prosecute, then it cannot be considered impartial. An independent judicial panel should decide if a prosecution is in the public interest, not a politician.

Trial by Jury

If the decision is taken to prosecute a Whistle-blower, then they should be tried by a jury in an open court.

Any decision to prosecute a Whistle-blower should be tested by the process of a fair hearing.

Clive Ponting was an assistant secretary in The Ministry of Defence who discovered that the Government had misled the House of Commons over the sinking of the Argentinian battleship the General Belgrano. Clive Ponting was prosecuted under The Official Secrets Act as it stood at that time, which banned Ponting from making such a disclosure unless it was to someone "to whom it is his duty in the interests of state to communicate the information."

Ponting admitted that he had leaked the information but argued that he was justified in doing so because it was in the interests of the state that such information be disclosed to an MP. This argument was flatly rejected by the judge, who stated that the "interests of the state" simply meant "of the Government of *the day*" and directed the jury **not** to allow Ponting's defence. The jury ignored this direction and acquitted Ponting, causing major embarrassment to the Government. This case raises the question, **why** did the Attorney General decide to prosecute and was it an impartial decision?

Justice and the law can be two very **different things**; a jury is the best hope of them being the **same thing**.

The Internal Route
Law Commission page 178, 7.83 "According to research conducted by Savage, the total number of approaches civil servants have made to the Civil Service Commission has remained low since it gained the **power to investigate***. For example, between March 2014 and April 2015, the Commission dealt with* **four cases***. Savage attributes these low numbers to two factors, first many of the complaints made to the Commission concern* **human resources issues** *which it rejects on the basis that the Civil Service Code precludes it from considering such matters. Secondly Savage suggests that the Commission's own guidance* **steers prospective complainants towards internal departmental and agency complaint mechanism**Firstly, I should point out that whistle-blowing is described as a "human Resources issue" because PIDA wrongly classes it

as an employment issue so that, as stated above, such issues cannot be investigated. In effect those individuals that are **most likely** to be Whistle-blowers and **most likely** in need of an effective internal route are the very people **refused** an effective investigation.

There are numerous references throughout the Law Commission Consultation document about using internal procedures such as the staff counsellor or the Civil Service Commission as a means of addressing concerns without resorting to public disclosure. It is not surprising these routes are rightly seen by Whistle-blowers as entirely ineffective because **they are used to divert attention from the concerns being raised**, and to suggest that the only problem is the employee.

The concept of internal reporting refers to PIDA, The Public Interest Disclosure Act as a source of guidance but PIDA is a completely flawed law. The Prescribed Regulator model has been proven beyond doubt to be entirely ineffective due to either being totally inadequate, incompetent, or in the few cases where they have effectively investigated and upheld concerns, their findings have been disregarded in PIDA judgments such as the case of the BUPA 7.

There are also a significant number of cases coming to our attention where a prescribed regulator such as the CQC has informed the employer of a Whistle-blower's identity.

It is therefore completely unrealistic to rely on a prescribed body or investigator in any sector, and even more so where Whistle-blowers face such a high risk of criminal prosecution for disclosing information in the public interest. That is why Edna's Law is **not** based on the prescribed regulator or investigatory commissioner model, but on three effective stages.

However, when a Whistle-blower discloses information, then assessing the effectiveness of the internal whistle-blowing route or any circumstances that led up to a Whistle-blower by-passing the internal route, should be considered. These are the initial issues that should be covered:

Is the Whistle-blower raising **convenient** or **inconvenient** issues?

Take account of **any** possible incentive to cover-up the issues.

Take account of the work record of the employee **prior** to whistle-blowing, and also any attempts to smear or discredit the person **after** the first time they raised concerns internally.

Take account of the track record of the employer i.e. how have they treated other Whistle-blowers and what action was taken on reported concerns?

Consider situations where the internal route is being by-passed because for example, any of the concerns being raised by the Whistle-blower are of such a serious nature that the Whistle-blower reasonably believes an **imminent** or on-going harm or risk of harm to others is involved. Or that the employer could be implicated in the wrong-doing or may have **prior knowledge** of the wrong-doing by any act or any failure to act.

Would the nature of the wrongdoing be a **motive** for an employer to discredit or cause detriment to the Whistle-blower?

What motive has the Whistle-blower in raising the concerns? e.g. Had they **anything** to gain by the disclosures? Why would they risk whistle-blowing?

What action was taken to address the wrongdoing? Is that action proportionate given the nature of the wrongdoing?

*Law Commission Consultation Page 151 6.42 "Lord Hope then proceeded to make the following comments, "As I see it, the scheme of the Act (OSA) is vulnerable to criticism on the ground that it lacks the necessary degree of sensitivity. There must as I have said, **be some doubt** as to whether a **Whistle-blower** who believes that he has good grounds for asserting that abuses are being perpetrated by the security or intelligence services will be able to persuade those to whom he can make disclosures to take his allegations seriously, to persevere with them and to effect changes which, if there was substance in them, are necessary" Law Commission Consultation 7.85 "although it is used infrequently, something which is perhaps attributable to its own guidance, a process does exist that enables concerns from civil servants to be investigated by independent statutory commissioners. **We believe that this satisfies the** *public interest* *as it means allegations of impropriety can be investigated and* ***ultimately resolved****.*

The Law Commission have not provided **any** figures for "**the resolved impropriety**". Given both the total numbers of civil servants and possible numbers of **"resolved concerns"** I would have expected at least a moderate number of case prosecutions for wrong-doing via this route, **if** it were truly effective. I would ask the Law Commission to publish the full data on the numbers of concerns reported and what resulting action was taken during the last ten years in order to assess this. Meanwhile I remain **doubtful that this route would satisfy anyone's idea of meeting the public interest**.

The security services have their own staff counsellor, who has handled **149**
cases since **1987**. That is only just over **3** a year.
However, I also note that in chapter 7 of the Law Commission Consultation a number of schemes are suggested, and repeated reference is made to **Dealing with complaints**. Whistle-blowers **never** make complaints - they raise **concerns**.

My concern is that using terminology such as "complaints" or "grievances" implies an attitude of either ignorance or intolerance towards whistle- blowers and an attempt to characterise the Whistle-blower as a problem employee.

"The Law Commission Consultation page 179, 7.85
"Although it is used infrequently, something which is perhaps attributable to its own guidance, a process does exist that enables concerns from civil servants to be investigated by independent statutory commissioners. ***We believe that this satisfies the public interes****t as it means allegations of impropriety can be investigated and ultimately resolved."*

There is **no evidence** to support the above claim, in fact **all** the evidence points in the very opposite direction. The above judgment by the Law Commission would not meet **most** people's idea of **satisfying the Public Interest.**

"The Law Commission Consultation Page 179 7.88 "In addition to these office holders, there are a number of

*processes which exist, and which are available to a member of the security and intelligence agencies who has concerns relating to their work. A **tiered regime** is in operation, in the sense that concerns are **first raised internally** but then can be raised with someone who is independent of the agency in question."*

Whistle-blowers from all sectors who report specific concerns internallyand then take those **same** concerns to any independent investigatory agency are identified by this **very act**. When an employee **also** discloses an employer's failure to act it will cost a person their livelihood for examples see, beyond the Façade, Edna's Law recognises this fact as it is based on comprehensive evidence.

The Law Commission consultation however concludes that the **more** people you approach internally, i.e. "the tiered regime", as being an effective route when **our evidence** points to this route resulting in **smearing or discrediting of Whistle-blowers**. The result is that disclosures of wrong-doing are **never** dealt with at all.

No one **chooses** to be a Whistle-blower, it is something they are forced to do by circumstances, an act of conscience in response to a wrong-doing that they cannot justify or turn a blind eye to. Whistle-blowing in any sector results in punishment from employers who are beyond the law. Blowing the whistle already costs people their jobs, future, and all hope. To place a Whistle-blower in a prison cell for committing an act of conscience is not only abhorrent, it is **such a grave injustice that it undermines public confidence in the justice system.**

Public Interest Defence for Whistle-blowers
*Law Commission Consultation Page 155 6.60 "In **Guja v Moldova** the applicant disclosed to a newspaper internal letters that demonstrated **political interference** with decisions whether to **prosecute individuals** for criminal offences. When it was discovered that he was the source of the disclosures, **the applicant was dismissed from his job in the Prosecutor General's Office**. This is not therefore a case in which the discloser of the information was prosecuted for a criminal offence, however the European Court of Human rights has relied upon the principles*

*articulated in Guja v Moldova in subsequent criminal case*The case of Guja v Moldova raises a number of issues:

Any prosecution of this Whistle-blower (Mr Guja) could only have confirmed the political interference with such decisions. This brings us back to our objections on the role of the Attorney General, which is a political appointment.
Were those involved in the wrong-doing ever held to account for perverting the course of justice and **if not**, why not?
Did the Whistle-blower pursue his/her case via the domestic courts and how long did he suffer financial hardship for the act of protecting others?
What were the other individuals accused of and why were they being prosecuted?

*"Law Commission Consultation Page 155 "The public interest in the disclosed information-The Grand Chamber stated that the interest which the public may have in particular information can sometimes be so strong so as to **over-ride even a legally imposed duty of confidence**. The court did not however provide further elucidation of what the term "Public Interest" means in this context, how it ought to be assessed or by whom."*

Defining the term **Public Interest** seems to cause much difficulty as opposed to the term, **National Interest** which encounters no such difficulty. Surely these two interests should run parallel. The further apart they are is a greater indication that something is very wrong.
A list of examples of what would be considered a Public Interest Disclosure should form part of a **separate public consultation**. I can think of no-one better qualified than the **public** to ask what is in their **interests**. This would address the argument about legal certainty and therefore **would allow a Public Interest Defence.**

*"Law Commission Consultation page 160 7.3 "At the outset it is necessary to point out that there are two versions of **public interest defence** that may be envisaged. The first type would require an assessment of whether the disclosure was in fact in the public interest. The second type would*

require an assessment of whether the defendant had a **genuine belief** *that the disclosure would
be in the public interest. Strictly speaking only, the former
constitutes a true public interest defence. Given that the latter
is not in fact concerned with the public interest, but rather
with what the defendant believed to be in the public interest.
Both of these formulations will be considered when
evaluating the merits of introducing a public interest defence"*

My view is that a public interest defence **must** be included. In
my experience one of the many failures of The Public Interest
Disclosure Act (PIDA) is that it relies on the "**reasonable
belief**" model which is flawed as will be explained below:
Firstly, PIDA has been misused and this has allowed a
number of cases to succeed with **questionable or even no**
public interest elements to the detriment of all **genuine**
Whistle-blowers.

Secondly the **reasonable belief** element shifts the focus in
judgments onto the individual rather than onto the evidence
of disclosure.

All genuine Whistle-blowers want the wrong-doing or abuses
dealt with and all the evidence on the disclosures examined
and judged. Edna's Law would provide this. Genuine
Whistle-blowers do not "**reasonably believe"** they are
acting in the public interest; **they know they are**. Edna's
Law will include a comprehensive list of examples of what is
a true public interest disclosure in every sector, negating the
need for "reasonable belief" which relies not on evidence but
on subjective opinions, of the defence, the prosecution and
the jury.

Law Commission Consultation page 162 7.12 "Our
preliminary consultation with Stakeholders
confirmed **(the Public Interest) Defence is pleaded very
rarely"**

*Law Commission Consultation page 167 7.32 "The
argument that is often made is that if an individual cannot
make a disclosure to the public in the knowledge that they
could plead a defence that the disclosure was in the public
interest if prosecuted, then the wrong-doing may never be
brought to light and may never be rectified. A public interest
defence could remedy this by encouraging an individual to*

make a public disclosure safe in the knowledge that they could plead that the disclosure was in the public interest if prosecuted, of course as discussed they could have no way of knowing in advance whether a jury would agree with their assessment that the disclosure was in the public interest. The existence of a public interest defence does not eliminate this risk"

Law Commission Consultation 7.63 "secondly the lack of clarity surrounding the concept of public interest would open the floodgates. Virtually anyone who wishes to raise the defence in relation to a charge of unauthorised disclosure could do so, notwithstanding the circumstances in which the offence was committed. If the public interest was a defence to unauthorised disclosure, it seems that no information could necessarily be guaranteed to be safe"

If the defence is **rarely pleaded** it is because whistle-blowing is rarely done lightly. The Law Commission consultation accepts this defence is **rarely** pleaded. Yet they go on to state that allowing such a defence would amount to "**opening the floodgates."** Whistle-blowers will be risking their careers and face long term financial hardship; these very large obstacles are a consideration also. Having a non-exhaustive list of what is "a Public Interest Disclosure" would also give clarity. With regard to the jury being a risk? The jury in Clive Ponting's case delivered a **just** if **inconvenient** verdict.

Public Interest Defence for Journalists
"Law Commission Consultation page 177 7.75 "In addition it is our view that the introduction of a statutory public interest defence solely for journalists could be considered arbitrary, given that there are other professionals who might violate the law in the pursuit of their legitimate activities."

I do not agree, firstly because it would not be "arbitrary" if Whistle-blowers were **also** afforded this defence. How can they violate the law if the activity is legitimate?
Secondly, the scope which this proposed legislation has to suppress information could easily be extended to include **any information** about **anything,** Government departments,

local authorities, private companies, prisons, the list is endless. The Law Commission Consultation relies on the conclusions of the Leverson inquiry.

As an organisation that supports both Whistle-blowers and the families of those who have suffered abuse, avoidable death and negligence, our aim is to break the chain that allows **all** abuse: i.e. complacency, ignorance, denial and most of all, silence. We work closely with the media to expose both the abuse and the failures of the authorities to act.

We are already seeing the negative impact of the **Leveson Inquiry** on the work we do with the media to expose abuse, it has become harder to get stories printed**, not** because there is any lack of evidence but because **just** the **threat** of legal proceedings has become a much more effective method to stop the truth being printed. The menace of costs has been used effectively to silence or punish Whistle-blowers. The threat of costs against the **winning side** in a libel case is yet another attack on free speech and is against natural justice. There needs to be the right balance in protecting people from invasion of privacy but also in protecting people by exposing abuse.

Law Commission Consultation page 131 "In Scott v Scott Lord Shaw of Dunfermline described **publicity in the administration of justice as one of the surest guarantees of our liberties."**

Law Commission Consultation Page 76 3.124 "In the case of Katharine Gun who disclosed information that came into her possession during the course of her work at GCHQ, the defence suggested that Ms Gun also intended to plead necessity as a defence. The CPS offered no evidence against Ms Gun, which meant that the prosecution was halted before the judge had to evaluate whether to leave the defence to the jury."

Law Commission Consultation page 77 "Duress is generally accepted in legal terms to be an excuse whereas necessity is generally seen to be a justification. Duress can be pleaded as a defence under the Official Secrets Acts 1989"

The defence of necessity should be allowed for Whistle-blowers.
The case of Catherine Gun shows that the Attorney General **cannot** be relied on for **impartiality.** There are cases that clearly warrant this defence.

Conclusion

The public perception of The Official Secrets Act is that it applies only to the intelligence agencies and top-secret information. However, our concern is that much of the information which this proposed law aims to protect has no bearing on the national interest. For example, many medical staff employed by Government departments would be asked to sign the OSA and therefore if there was a need to whistle-blow about abusive conditions or negligent.
Noel Finn a nurse working at Yarls Wood Detention Centre is a prime example because he was asked to sign the OSA and refused.
When is a Crime not a Crime?
The judge ruled in Clive Ponting's case that the interests of the state simply meant the **interests of the Government of the day**. Because the Law Commission has included and relied on legislation from several countries including the United States, we ask this question:
If for example, a security service in the USA leaks negative information about their own **Government of the day** and this is **not** treated as a criminal offence. but a Whistle-blower from the USA is imprisoned for the same reason, would this not undermine the administration of justice?
So, the answer to "When is a crime not a crime?" appears to be "When it suits those in power".
Police Whistle-blowers should be fully consulted regarding the measures needed to specially protect police. A number of Police whistle-blowers and campaigners follow us on twitter, the measures they call for are supported by us.

Edna's Law The Disclosures

Of the following examples, some are entirely fictional, and the remainder may relate in part to actual events but all identifying information has been removed. The following examples are not an exhaustive list by any means, they are just a small example of the evidence we have available which will be fully included in Edna's Law Part Three, The Disclosure Index.

John

John is a security Guard working nights and patrols an office building randomly:

He carries a bleeper which would alert him to any breech of security that may occur regardless of where he was in the building. John's line manager asks John to empty a small amount of litter bins during his shift. John refuses to comply with this and is given a written warning by his employer. John continues to refuse to carry out this duty and is eventually dismissed. John then claims to be a Whistle-blower, stating that he informed his employer that the duties he was asked to carry out would put the building security at risk.

This is not whistle-blowing but is a work grievance, so it would not be protected under Edna's Law.
Why? Because John is patrolling an empty building which is locked and secured. His duties are to randomly patrol the building and therefore it is obvious that regardless of where John was on the site or what he was doing, the pager he carried would alert him to any risk. Therefore, the duty in dispute, namely the emptying of bins did not and would not impact on public safety. The rights or wrongs of his work grievance are **not** relevant to whistle-blowing.

Peter

Peter works as a security guard at a TV broadcaster, his duties consist of

sitting at a reception and vetting visitors who need to enter the building,

issuing visitors passes

checking people in and out for security and fire emergency purposes.

Peter is asked to leave his post unattended and help his line manager move some desks and chairs in another part of the building.

Peter says he cannot do that unless there is someone else who will take his place at the front desk as leaving his post would mean that anyone could enter the building and it was a dangerous thing to allow. Peter's line manager is not happy with this and storms off.

Later that day Peter writes out a report of his concerns and takes this report to the CEO of the company. This report states that in the event of a fire no one would know exactly who was in the building. Peter also highlights that during his training he was told that a TV studio could be a target for terrorists because of its editorial stance or because terrorists could draw a lot of attention to their cause from such an attack. Similar situations had arisen at other broadcasters.

Peter states he does not want to be awkward but is concerned that he may be asked to leave his post again or that one of the other team members on entrance security may also encounter such a situation. He asks that it is made clear to all staff that reception security must be manned at all times.

Three days later Peter is called to a meeting attended by HR and told serious allegations have been made against him by his line manager, who has reported Peter for being verbally abusive and not a team player.

Peter explains about the whistleblowing but is ignored and in the weeks that follow Peter's colleagues send him to Coventry as they have been told he complained about everyone.

Peter eventually dreads going to work as his line manager continually asks him to leave his post and when he refuses to do this, reports Peter for misconduct.

A short while later Peter was signed off sick by his GP and he never returns to work.

This IS whistle blowing

Why? Because Peter was asked to complete a task that would have resulted in a serious breach of security and which could have placed everyone working or visiting that building at risk of harm. Peter is motivated by the risk to public safety and clearly states this to the CEO.

The subsequent harassment could have been prevented had the CEO taken the action Peter requested. The action requested is reasonable in all the circumstances. The concerns were reasonable in all the circumstances.

The foreseeable risk highlighted by Peter could incur serious harm to the public interest in that over 200 people worked in the building and many more visited and all these individuals were owed a clear duty of care, to work or visit a safe environment, where any identifiable risks had been reasonably negated, the risk of harm identified by Peter was a continual risk.

Edna's Law will provide the information a Whistle-blower needs to make a notification. See Step 1 which ensures that all those who are **not** genuine Whistle-blowers are filtered out at this very early stage thus saving time and resources for those who are genuine Whistle-blowers.

See Step 2 for clear timescales for the employer/accountable person to act according to disclosure type. Unlike the EU Whistleblowing Law, which beggars' belief by placing a timeframe of three months for action on **everything.**

These first two steps ensure the Whistle-blower is protected because Edna's Law has a clear set of procedures that ensures, **everyone knows what is required**, **what is acceptable and what is not**.

This leaves no room for manoeuvre by employers pleading the Whistle-blower did not tell them and most importantly allows the police to intervene at an exact point because the failure to act has been evidenced by the unique systems set out in Edna's Law which result in the risk of harm being made safe.

So, when Peter informed his employer in writing of his concerns then one of three things can occur:

A The employer takes the action requested within the time limit because Edna's Law is an effective deterrent and the employer does not want to face the consequences. This results in Peter keeping his job, never facing hardship and harassment and most importantly for everyone working or visiting the building being safe from every foreseeable risk.

B The employer takes action to address the concerns, but Peter is subsequently harassed. Peter reports this and the employer takes immediate action to protect Peter, because Edna's Law makes harming a Whistle-blower by allowing harassment or other detriment a criminal offence and the employer does not want to face the consequences of breaking the law.

C The employer fails to act on the whistleblowing and/or the subsequent harassment or detrimental treatment and is prosecuted under Edna's Law. Peter is compensated for all losses incurred or likely to be incurred, thus adding to those cases that act as a deterrent to other employers.

The outcomes in **A** and **B** are the aims of Edna's Law, but these outcomes will **only** happen when enough cases of **C** are prosecuted. The only way to change culture is to have such an effective deterrent.

The CEO in Peter's case will face the most serious breach, the line manager and HR officers will also face charges. (See part two for full details)

Edna's Law ensures both the public's and the Whistle-blower's safety from the point of failure to act, because if the time limit for action is not met then the Whistle-blower can go straight to the police who will refer them to the new Public Interest Crime Unit. This unit will have minimum investigation requirements

Edna's law picks up the genuine Whistle-blower in their workplace and carries them over every hurdle, from the beginning to justice and accountability whilst PIDA just leaves them to sink without trace.

Examples of what are and are not protected disclosures and why

Jane

Jane is a care worker who reports to her manager that she is not able to take the breaks she is entitled to. This is **not** whistleblowing but a work grievance.

Why? There is no mention of any risk to others, there is clear reference to Jane's entitlements as an employee, but there is no identifiable public interest motive for raising the concern.

Minal

Minal is a care worker and reports that she is unable to take any breaks because if she took her break it would result in residents being at risk of harm. Minal states the harm she foresees as a result of her taking a break as leaving only one staff on duty, when two staff are required to carry out duties such as hoisting.

This IS whistle blowing

Why? Because Minal's motive in reporting these concerns is risk to others. Also consider:

The conditions will be repeated numerous times on each shift.

That other less conscientious staff members maybe be taking their breaks so there is a perceived as well as an actual risk of harm.

Did the employer fully consider and investigate all the implications of harm?

Does this home have a history of incidents that could be related this disclosure?

Please note CQC inspection reports are **not** admissible as an authority of evidence under Edna's law and can only be considered in terms of content and not judgments or ratings. For example, a home being rated good is not reliable evidence. But if in the body of an inspection report it is recorded that a member of staff raised concerns about staffing levels that information is admissible, regardless of whether CQC ignored the fact in their overall rating. CQC are not a recognised authority by Edna's Law

David

David reports that the company he works for is using substandard scaffolding bolts, which do not fit correctly and are snapping off.

David reports this to his line manager, when no action is taken, he follows it up and reports further incidents where bolts have snapped off. When David sees that no action is being taken within the timeline under Edna's Law, he can contact the police at this point.

Under PIDA David is left to take his concerns to the board of the company, which results in him being moved around the construction site and asked to do tasks he's untrained to complete until he is finally called to a disciplinary hearing and told his work is substandard.

Edna's Law considers the following:

Eileen Chubb

The issues that David reported related to a risk of serious injury or death
David had nothing to gain by reporting the concerns
The faulty scaffolding places all employees at serious risk of injury or death, this risk extends to members of the public you may be passing by the site
The failure to act on serious concerns has to be taken as a companywide failure which means that not just the one construction site may be affected but all current and future sites and employees and members of the public coming into contact with those current or future sites.
Other employees are deterred from reporting concerns after seeing how David is treated by the company which impact on other areas of safety and risk.
The potential harm to people, the family and friends impacted by a loved one's death or serious injury is fully recognised in Edna's Law.

The scale of such impact is not currently assessed at all, Edna's Law would recognise and consider the following:
A circle of abusers working in a home,

Abuser number one is a power abuser (link see beyond the facade) has worked in social care for 17 years, is 24 years old and unless identified and removed will continue to work until 65 **Opportunity for future abuse? 41 years.**
Abuser number two is a complacency abuser, is 36 years old and has worked in care for 10 years and unless identified and removed will continue to work. **Opportunity for future abuse? 29 years.**
Abuser number three is an ignorance abuser and unless identified and retrained will continue to harm. They are 29 years old and have worked in care one year and will continue to work. **Opportunity for future abuse? 36 years**
Abuser number four is a power abuser and is 37 years old, has worked in care 10 years and unless identified and removed will continue to work. **Opportunity for future abuse? 28 years.**
Abuser number 5 is a look the other way abuser, he is 40 years old and a senior manager so unless he is identified and removed, he will continue to allow people to be harmed

by abusive staff and will allow the harassment of any Whistle-blowers who report it. Unless identified and removed will have the **opportunity to continue to allow abuse and silence Whistle-blowers for another 25 years How many people would have the above have harmed previously?**
How many people will they be able to continue to harm in future?
Thousands
How many Whistle-blowers need to speak out under the protection of Edna's Law to remove all of the above?
Just one.

Richard
Richard is a trainee chef who sees out of date food being routinely served to hotel guests and reports this.
This is Whistle-blowing

Barry
Barry is a trainee chef and complains to management that he thinks staff should be able to take leftover food home.
This is **not** whistle-blowing

Magdalena
A care home manager instructs staff to write false witness statements and falsify care plans in order to evict a resident from a care home on the pretext they cannot meet the resident's needs, when really it is because the person's daughter has raised concerns about specific staff members' conduct. Magdalena refuses to write this and reports the manager.
This is whistle-blowing

Carla
A care worker complains that her manager is asking staff to pay 50p if they have a meal.
This is **not** whistle-blowing

Tom
Tom is a firefighter who discovers there is a lack of specialist equipment in certain situations and he reports this.
This is whistle-blowing

Tony
Tony works on a building site and is asked to make cups of tea for other workers and refuses to do this as it is not in his contract.
This is **not** whistle-blowing

Miguel
Is a truck driver and he sees a fellow driver drinking vodka on duty and reports this.
This is whistle-blowing

Alyson
Alyson works in the HR department of a pharmaceutical company. She is asked to write to an employee of the company regarding the persons conduct. A disciplinary meeting is arranged where it emerges that the staff member being disciplined is a Whistle-blower and is being victimised. Alyson refuses to take part in this and reports the manager involved.
This is Whistle-blowing.

Marco
Marco is a freelance journalist working on an investigation piece about a celebrity who has abused underage girls, for a news broadcaster. The story is not broadcast, and Marco discovers that strings have been pulled to stop the story. Marco reports this.
This is whistle-blowing

Roman
Roman is a truck driver who discovers that his employer is storing hazardous waste in a depot instead of disposing of it. The waste is leaking into the soil. Roman reports this.

This is whistle-blowing

Edward
Edward is a truck driver who raises concerns with his employer about his sat nav not being updated which is inconvenient and making him late sometimes.
This is **not** whistle-blowing

Laura
Laura sees a restaurant manager refreezing food that had thawed out after a freezer broke down. This food was discoloured and smelt. The temperature chart on the freezer was also falsified. Laura questions the manager but is told to stay quiet and she then reports this to the owner.
This is whistle-blowing

Sara
Works in a bakery and reports her manager for selling burnt bread.
This is **not** whistle-blowing.

Niels
Niels is a journalist working at a local newspaper who writes a story about abuse at a local home which is backed up with evidence and many witnesses but the story is spiked because the owner of the care home in question is the newspaper's main advertiser and the paper cannot afford to lose the revenue. Niels reports this.
This is whistle-blowing.

Amanda
Amanda is a social worker and reports her concerns that her case load is too large, and she cannot spend the time she needs to protect children at risk.

This is whistle-blowing.
Frank
 Frank is a social worker and is told to place clients at a particular care home that is known to be bad. Frank says he will try to find alternative places for his clients, but his manager says not to spend any more time on this and send them to the bad home.
This is whistle-blowing

Hans
Hans works for a car manufacturer and discovers a new model's emissions data is being falsified. Hans reports this.
This is whistle-blowing

Simon
Simon works for a furniture manufacturer and discovers the foam being used in sofas is not flame resistant but a cheaper version which is flammable. Simon reports this.
This is whistle-blowing

Sandra
Sandra works in a care home and sees another care worker hit an elderly resident and she reports this
This is Whistle-blowing

Pierre
Works in a plastic bottle factory. Pierre discovers that the plastic rings which are supposed to secure the bottle lid on opening are faulty and he reports this.
This is whistle-blowing

Ian
Works in a packaging factory. Ian thinks he should be paid more than Pete who works alongside him and who he suspects may be getting an extra bonus.
This is **not** whistle-blowing

Tibot
Works for the CPS and discovers several cases are to be prosecuted which involve evidence being withheld which would exonerate the suspects. Tibot reports this.
This is whistle-blowing

Sally
Sally works at a bank and discovers that customers are being overcharged and she reports this.
This is whistle-blowing

Amy
Amy works for a loan company and discovers that customers are being overcharged on interest rates. She reports this.
This is whistle-blowing

Delyth
Delyth works for the NHS and is concerned the staffing levels on the ward she is on are too low and placing patients at risk.
This is whistle-blowing

Any issue in relation to patient care is protected.

Marcia
Marcia is a probation officer who reports her caseload of high-risk offenders is too large and is placing public safety at risk
This is whistle-blowing

Christine
Christine is a teacher and raises concerns about the misuse of funds by the head mistress who has used school funds to buy several expensive items for her son.
This is whistle-blowing

Alex
Is an official at a public inquiry into deaths at a hospital. Alex discovers that certain evidence is being concealed from the inquiry report which is vital to the outcome and Alex reports this.
This is whistle-blowing

This list is but a very small selection and **Edna's Law Part 3 The Disclosure Directory** will be a comprehensive guide to protected disclosures.

Summary on Protected Disclosures
In summer 2017 I were asked to speak about whistle-blowing at Birkbeck University Political Studies Department on whistle-blowing. I arranged for a panel of Whistle-blowers to speak consisting of
Eileen Chubb   Social Care whistle-blower
Christine England NHS and social care Whistle-blower
Karis Le Winton   The Old Deanery Whistle-blower featured in Panorama
Joe Koskow   Home care whistle-blower

After the sessions for the day finished there was a general discussion, with the other panellists who included an academic "expert" Dr Wim Vandekerckhove.
He gave the following example as typical whistle-blowing,

"A security guard went to work each day and when he went to make a cup of tea found the sink full of washing up, which he washed up. The security guard then raised this with his manager, saying he should not have to wash up. At the next meeting the security staff were told they had to wash up their own cups as X had complained"

Dr Wim Vandekerckhove considered this whistle-blowing as it was about teamwork. **So is rugby but it's not whistle-blowing**.
I told him that he was trivialising whistle-blowing and the security guard chose to wash up and the whole situation was petty, and no lives were at risk from dirty cups. He strongly disagreed.
I gave the following examples to demonstrate what is and is **not** whistle-blowing.
A person has a broken leg and goes to work but does not have enough leg room at her desk, she complains and calls this whistle-blowing on the grounds the public would be outraged at how her leg had been treated.
B A crane driver on a construction site raises a concern that he does not have enough elbow room to operate the controls safely and there is a real risk of dropping heavy loads as a result
I said that example B was a Whistle-blower as he was reporting something that put people at risk and not something about his comfort levels.
I pointed out that Example A was a real PIDA case and was judged to be whistle-blowing.

Chapter Nine,
The 13 Steps

Step 1:   Staff Know They Are Protected
The Statutory Notice

(Please note: The below are core components, the full notice and whistle-blower pack will be published in Part Two)

The Rule of Law requires that there can be no punishment without law. This notice ensures that all employers/accountable persons are aware of their responsibilities and the liabilities for breaches of those responsibilities. This step ensures there is no ignorance of the law.

There can be no legal protection without knowledge that protection exists. This step ensures that knowledge and guidance is available to all protected persons, by the following method.

As with the Statutory Notice the Health and Safety at Work Act, which is displayed in all work premises, Edna's Law will utilise the positive aspects of such a notice but will go further.

The negative aspects of the Health and Safety at Work Act Statutory notice.

Because of the language used and presentation and content of the information, I would venture very few people have read all of this notice, and even fewer will have understood it.

This notice does not give advice as to where further information could be accessed.

It makes no allowance for those who do not understand legal jargon.

It does not make it relevant to those who it protects by not stating what you are supposed to do if there is a breach.

It makes no allowance for those who may struggle with literacy issues or language barriers.

It does not utilise the digital interactive technology of today's world.

Positive Aspects
It is a Government issued notice required by law to be displayed.
It is uniform in content and cannot be watered down to a barely compliant version that is more convenient for the employer.
It is part of the workplace and recognised if not always understood.

The Edna's Law Statutory Notice and Protected Persons Information Pack

This is not red tape but a lifeline to those who Whistle-blowers act to protect.
A Government-issued notice on Edna's Law protections to be displayed in all areas used by protected persons.
That every protected person is provided with a copy of the Protected Persons Pack which is available for employers and accountable persons to easily download from the Edna's Law section of the Government website.
That any breach of the above is always penalised by a fine of not less than two thousand pounds for each separate breach.
That each breach is published in full on the PICU website as a resource for transparency. The fines are used to provide Whistle-blower assistance as referred to below.

Content of the Statutory Notice and Pack

Both the notice and pack must be written in plain English.
The first line must state that Edna's Law protects you if you need to blow the whistle. It also informs you that false allegations have a penalty.
Both the notice, which needs to be posted and the information packs which are free to download can be accessed once the employer/accountable person types in the designated Whistle-blowing email address which is required by Edna's Law to be provided by every employer/accountable person and failure to provide this contact email will result in a fine of not less than £2000.
All breaches will be published in full on the aforementioned website.

The information pack must be provided to every protected person.

This information pack will provide a copy of the statutory notice.

A copy of the Whistle-blowing form

A copy of the reporting harassment or detriment form

What is/not whistle-blowing information

Basic information about harassment and detriment as a result of whistle-blowing

A link to the government website where the information can be accessed in other languages

A phone number to contact if you need to ask for assistance because you have a literacy or language or disability barrier

Information about why it is so important to record in writing your Whistle-blowing

This first step ensures that no employer/accountable person can plead ignorance of the law.

All fines for breaches pay for the assistance that must be provided to Whistle-blowers at each step.

That no protected person is denied the basic information they need to access the protection of Edna's Law.

That no protected person is denied this information because they have a literacy or language barrier or visual impairment or other needs.

That those individuals who are **not genuine** Whistle-blowers are filtered out at a very early stage, allowing all resources to be targeted on the genuine.

Edna's Law STEP TWO: Whistle-blowing

Please note the full pack and procedures will be detailed in Part Two.

Giving the information that the employer/accountable person needs to act on.

Whilst most people find form-filling difficult the following method has to be used because it ensures:

That the Whistle-blower can report their concerns so that action can be taken.

If those concerns are not subsequently acted on then there is a clear paper trail that takes that failure to act to the threshold for a criminal prosecution to succeed, beyond all reasonable doubt.

This process protects the Whistle-blower so that the date and time of the whistle-blowing are clearly logged, and any subsequent detrimental treatment can be clearly linked. This form will be in each protected person's Edna's Law pack, so they do not have to go to the employer/accountable person and ask for this at a very stressful and traumatic time or draw attention to the fact that are going outside the organisation, which would put them at risk.

The protected person who needs assistance in filling in this form will have the contact details of where that assistance can be obtained.
 The form will be kept simple but must include the following;
An assurance that the employer/accountable person has a legal duty to protect the Whistle-blower's identity and ensure they are safe from any harassment.
These are general requirements of content and detail can be added but the crucial content is not negotiable.
These examples are not intended to cover all whistle-blowing situations, just those that need to be highlighted as a priority at the top of this form so the employer can see imminent risk situations at glance.
Tick this box if there is an imminent danger of loss of life or serious injury (do you need to contact the emergency services at this point or is it an issue only your employer can act upon?
Vulnerable people are being abused
A criminal offence is being or is likely to be committed.
Patient care is being compromised.
Unsafe practices are taking place.
Any other urgent situation enter details below.
General sections to cover all other areas.
List your concerns as briefly as you can here.
You ask your employer/accountable person to take a full statement from you by ticking this box
Is there any documentation or other evidence that will assist your employer/accountable person to investigate? List this below.
Are there any witnesses, should your employer interview all staff, staff on a particular site or shift?
What harm is being done or could be done as result of these issues?

Why do you feel these issues need to be addressed?
What action do you expect to be taken?

EDNAS LAW, STEP THREE
TIMESCALES BY WHICH ACTION MUST BE TAKEN

This Step ensures both employer/accountable person and
the Whistle-blower know what to expect. It gives clear
timescales for the immediate action to be taken to make safe
a situation and a timescale for investigations to be
completed by.
Unlike the EU whistle-blowing law proposals which incredibly
give three months for everything, regardless of the particular
circumstances.
In contrast Edna's Law gives clear timescales for action
based on the risks involved.
I will start with an example that clearly demonstrates how
quickly a situation can be made safe if Edna's Law were in
force at the time.
There is a perception that if something is so wrong, so
dangerous, then surely action should have been taken,
however what happens when a Whistle-blower tells an
employer that this is wrong, a very different type of
behaviour can all too often be the response and Edna's Law
targets this behaviour.
An Edna's Law protected Whistle-blower informs his
employer that it is dangerous for ferries to sail with their bow
doors open.
There is an imminent danger of loss of life or serious injury.
Timescale for action to make the situation safe. **Before the
next ferry sails.**
This would involve the employer making at most three phone
calls to the ports involved and suspending services to
ensure all staff are aware that this practice must cease with
immediate effect.
The investigation into why this practice occurred, how
widespread it is and to issue a written alert. Timescale: **1
week.**

Now there are those who would argue that such a course of
action would cause major disruption to the public, my
response to this is:

If you issued a form to all those passengers waiting to board
the **Herald of Free Enterprise at Zeebrugge** and asked
them to tick one of two boxes:

Would you prefer to be delayed?

Or drowned?

The response to such a poll is my response.

**Edna's Law timescales for making safe and then
investigating**

Where there is an imminent danger of loss of life or serious
injury.

Timescale to make safe and secure evidence: 1 hour
**Timescale to investigate and alert relevant persons (i.e.
alert PICU) and issue notification: 1 week**

Where dangerous equipment is being used:

Timescale to make safe and secure evidence: 1 hour
**Timescale to investigate and alert relevant persons (i.e.
alert PICU) and put right: 1 week**

When vulnerable adults/children are being abused or placed
at risk

**Timescale to make safe 1 hour by suspending those
identified and secure evidence.**
**Timescale to investigate alert relevant persons (i.e. alert
PICU) and put right, 1 week.**

When patient care is being compromised

Timescale to make safe within 1 hour.
**Example Bristol heart surgery Whistle-blower Steven
Bolsin case.**

Suspend those implicated immediately. Secure evidence,
investigate, guided by the knowledge of the Whistle-blower,
who is qualified enough to know something is wrong and is
more than qualified to help put it right.

**Inform PICU, 2-week timeframe for investigation as
numbers of victims.**

In response to those who would say these timeframes are
too short. I would say that things are only ever complicated
when made so by a half-hearted or superficial investigation
which by their nature take far longer to gloss over the facts
to protect reputation than to actually deal with the facts.

The deterrent of Edna's Law will miraculously speed up such investigations. **When lives are at risk then the clock is ticking, and Edna's Law ensures every second counts because every single life counts.**
Financial wrong-doing and corruption: **12 hours to suspend any staff, Inform relevant bodies (i.e. alert PICU) and obtain investigation.**
Secure evidence. Investigate and action: 8 weeks.
Extension on timeframe can be applied for depending on circumstances.
If you are manufacturing any item that is a public safety risk:
2 hours to inform relevant authorities and 6 hours to do initial tests and issue public alert.
1 week to do all tests and issue product re-call.
All whistle-blowing that benefits an organisation such as financial loss due to theft, the time limit to investigate all "convenient" Whistle-blowing in this area is 2 months.
Any criminal offence: inform PICU within 1 hour

EDNAS LAW STEP FOUR
ASSESSING THE ACTION TAKEN

The employer is required to respond in writing to the Whistle-blower stating what evidence was considered in their investigation and a full account of what action has been taken as a result.
Edna's Law is aimed at those employers who deliberately fail to act. If any action that is taken is merely superficial and not reasonable in all the circumstances, then at this point the employer/accountable person can be reported to the PICU for failing to act. Failure to act is a criminal offence under Edna's Law and is liable on conviction to a minimum prison term of one year and a maximum term which will be detailed in Edna's Part 2, as well as a substantial fine and damages.
The whistle-blower takes both the initial whistle-blowing form and a copy of the employer's response to PICU.
The below extracts are from the barrister Ian Scott in relation to BUPAs investigation into the BUPA 7 Case and highlight failures to act that would meet the criminal threshold of Edna's Law. These are intended as a guide to enable an assessment of degree of failure to act. No two cases are the

same, but the measure should be: was the action taken reasonable in all the circumstances? Please note that "EP" referred to below is Edna to whom this law is dedicated.

"It is in the area of the administration of medication that objective evidence on which the reasonable beliefs as to malpractice were formed is clearest. In particular the statement of Eileen Chubb paragraphs 14; 31. 49 specific allegations are made"

"The Tribunal is asked is asked to find that the respondents (BUPA) consistent response to the applicants' complaints has been one of denial and unwillingness to accept that the applicants raised genuine concerns about the treatment of residents at Isard House. This was made evident throughout the hearing before the Tribunal by the way the case was put by the respondents (BUPA) in denying all the applicants' complaints and suggesting they had concocted their evidence"

"It is submitted that of direct relevance to such an assessment of reasonable belief in such allegations where there is corroborating witness or evidence e.g. witnessing a push in the back of a resident or other abusive behaviour where the effect is transitory)are other complaints made by the applicant where the Tribunal finds that there was evidence which shows that the subject matter of the complaints is demonstrated on the balance of probabilities and or beyond all reasonable doubt. It is submitted that such findings significantly add to the credibility of the applicant concerned and add weight to the …. for example, the Tribunals attention is drawn to the objective evidence of Eileen Chubb's complaints about failures in Maria Keenahan's administration of medication"

"..Such efforts are difficult to reconcile to Des Kelly's evidence to the Tribunal that assault of a resident would be regarded by the respondents as gross misconduct. Maria Keenahan had admitted assault of the resident BM to (the PIDA prescribed regulator) the RIU in her

interview with them (page 118 B4) as she did at the beginning of her cross examination BUPA do not appear to have taken the matter seriously at any stage as Maria Keenahan continues to be employed by them"

"At paragraph 31 of her statement to the Tribunal, Eileen Chubb referred to the treatment of EP (Edna) with excess amounts of chlorpromazine. She referred to this matter in her interview with the RIU on 22nd April 1999 (p.24 B4.)
An examination of the relevant MAR sheet demonstrates that this overdosing was being carried out. In particular pp32 and 33 Bundle 3 reflect the overdosing which was going on.
The Tribunal is asked to note at p33 that the label dated 21st April 1999 prescribing "4 to 6 x 5ml spoonsful of chlorpromazine to be taken three times daily was stuck over the label at p32 prescribing 4 x 5mls spoonful's three times a day. The Tribunal is also asked to note that this was being done on the day the prescribed regulator RIU entered the home to begin its investigation on 23rd April.
It is submitted that a reasonable interpretation of the act of sticking the label dated 21st April 1999 over the previous label is to hide the repeated unauthorised overdosing of chlorpromazine at a level of 30ml three times a day by Maria Keenahan.

When confronted by this evidence Maria Keenahan sought to argue it away by suggesting that she was merely carrying out what has previously properly been given the previous month. When the previous month's sheet was examined, (p31 B3), the label for the dosage was missing altogether. Further, when asked, Maria Keenahan was not sure what the dosage on the missing label was likely to have been and made a number of suggestions including lower doses than those recorded as being given.
The Tribunal is also referred to the notes of the investigatory interview held with Maria Keenahan by Des Kelly (author's note: he was later given the OBE) on

10th August 1999 (p173 B4) in which she indicates that she was judging what chlorpromazine to give.

Further, Eileen Chubb's concerns about the state of the MAR sheets on Unit 3 and the administration of medication on Unit 3 have been borne out by the independent pharmacist's report (pp43-48 B3) which was undertaken as part of the investigation by the RIU (prescribed regulator) and the Tribunal is particularly directed to the findings in the report in respect of EP at Item 5 (p45) and DH at item 14 (p46).
The aim of the Act (i.e. PIDA) was to ensure that where malpractice is reported in organisations such as BUPA the organisation's response should be to investigate and deal with the message being brought forward….
…. It has included as set out and detailed below, no investigation whatsoever of the Applicants' complaints of harassment and continued risk, an inadequate investigation of Maria Keenahan's behaviour and their surreptitious relocation of Maria Keenahan to work in other homes in Bromley despite the prescribed regulator's known opposition to their doing so.
Maria Keenahan continues to work for BUPA notwithstanding her admission of assault on a resident. It is furthermore submitted that in addition to issues concerning the health and safety of residents, the Applicants brought to their employers' attention that they had been subjected to harassment by fellow employees……in particular they did so directly to Des Kelly, the Respondent BUPA's regional director, at their meeting with him on 14th May 1999. At paragraph 35 of his witness statement Mr Kelly recalls that Eileen Chubb made reference to being pushed in the back by another member of staff. He did not recall any other members of staff making any specific allegations of harassment. In cross-examination when shown the colour-coding of the details of the staff, produced by the Applicants at their meeting with him on 14th May (pp738/739 B2), he accepted that it indicated that not only staff who were alleged to be abusing residents but also staff who were identified with harassment…..

"In addition to Carol Jones's inadequate investigation of poor medication procedures made in response to Eileen Chubb's complaint, the Respondent's subsequent investigation carried out by Susan Greenwood, Quality Assurance Manager, appears to have been equally inadequate. Des Kelly's evidence was that it resulted in few recommendations and that there were no major concerns (paragraph 42 of Des Kelly's witness statement). It is not until an <u>independent</u> survey was carried out that the extent of the failures to apply proper medication procedures became clear.

Such an inadequate response by the Respondent to such serious complaints can only be taken as a <u>deliberate</u> failure on their part to act on the complaints. Had the issues been taken seriously, with the resources they have the Respondents BUPA could equally well have obtained expert advice about the administration of medication in the same way that the RIU (the prescribed regulator) did, once matters had been formally raised with them by the Applicants."

Under Edna's Law this failure to act would be a criminal offence.

"When Eileen Chubb made a complaint to her (i.e. Carol Jones, manager) about Maria Keenahan's poor medication practice she made only a cursory snapshot examination of the position and found nothing serious to be concerned about. It is clear from the independent pharmacist's report (pp43-48 B3) and the evidence before the Tribunal of the content of MAR sheets in respect of EP and DH that there were serious problems related to the administration of medication. These included overdosing of EP by Maria Keenahan with chlorpromazine. A proper examination of the MAR sheets at the time would have revealed these failings. ..... The Respondent's attitude and approach to the Applicants, culminating as it has in their <u>blanket denial</u> of the Applicants' evidence before the Tribunal and suggestions of concoction and improper personal motives in pursuing their complaints, have aggravated and compounded the damage done to the Applicants

> *who genuinely raised the issues they did in the interests of protection of the residents at Isard House.....*
> The Applicants further submit that they made qualifying disclosures within the *meaning of s43H.*
> *The matters they were disclosing were <u>exceptionally serious failures</u> involving the health and safety of elderly and highly dependent individuals who were being abused and were likely to continue being abused were the disclosures not made. In all the circumstances it was reasonable for the Applicants to make their disclosures. .....*
> *Des Kelly's response to the Applicants' solicitor's letter of 7th June raising concerns about a safe working environment of the Applicants and harassment of them by other staff (p330) was an <u>immediate denial</u> by him of any responsibility on the part of the Respondents BUPA (p332), without any investigation or proper consideration of any concerns."*

If all the identical evidence in this case were put before a judge and jury in a criminal court, then without a shadow of a doubt BUPA would be convicted. That is the crucial difference in Edna's Law, accountability for failure to act. **Every individual, from line manager to CEO, who fails to act will be held accountable in a criminal court.** Absolute denial currently allows bad employers to escape justice under PIDA. That same denial is an aggravated offence under Edna's Law.

If your employer says they investigated and acted but what you see is

The abusive care worker still abusing

The fire door still blocked

The ferry still sailing with the bow door open

Patient safety still compromised

Dangerous practices still happening on the construction site

Then your employer, <u>because</u> your concerns have been logged in writing, has knowledge of the wrongdoing and intends to allow the wrongdoing to continue.

At this point the failure to act is a deliberate action and Edna's Law has paved the way for the Whistle-blower now to take this to the Public Interest Crime Unit (PICU) because

Edna's Law has laid the paper trail to beyond all reasonable doubt.

Minimum police investigation requirements on failure to act.

Care industry investigation example.

A care worker is asked by a nurse to write in a patient's care plan that the patient was aggressive or agitated that day. The care worker says she knows the patient well and has never known them to be aggressive. The nurse tells the care worker that this is in order for the GP to prescribe sedative medication. The care worker reports the nurse to the employer/accountable person. This is a public interest disclosure.

If this nurse is able to obtain medication by this method of deception then she is very likely to have used this method previously, and is likely to use this method in future, therefore no limits can be placed on how many patients may be affected. (If this approach had been taken at Gosport, hundreds of lives could have been saved.)
The risks of side effects from the medication should be weighed against the benefits of the medication. If the patient can gain no benefit, then only risk of harm is inflicted, and it is inflicted by using fraudulent paperwork.
As the risk of adverse side effects from this kind of medication are increased when for example the patient is elderly and has impaired renal clearance, in this case the death rates for the care home need to be looked at in depth and compared with a similar sized home of the same care category. The incident should not be looked at in isolation but investigated in order to obtain all the facts about the bigger picture.
Has this nurse been reported previously?
To whom and what action was taken in the past?
How many other staff were also asked to participate in falsifying care records?
Did these other staff falsify the care records when asked and why? (The investigating officer should give assurances that

these others are not in trouble themselves, but they need to tell the police officer the truth).

Did any of these other staff report the nurse?

How many patients are currently at risk and what external medical attention is needed?

Blood/urine tests should be obtained in order to secure evidence.

Under no circumstances can the care provider investigate themselves. Under no circumstances can a care provider's word be accepted without question.

The regulators in the UK, CQC in England and CSSIW in Wales are excluded from the process.

Investigation example: Care industry

One of the most common disclosures made by health care staff is in relation to staffing levels. This can include:

People being left in bed without care, food or drink, sometimes until midday from 8pm the previous night.

In such cases PICU must

Obtain impact assessment.

Obtain data for bed sores, dehydration and all other hospital admissions.

Obtain medical opinion about the impact on mental and physical state caused by sixteen-hour periods of total neglect.

People being moved by drag lifting as it is quicker than going to get a hoist can often be an indicator of low staffing levels. This needs to be investigated because people who need assistance to eat and drink may not be getting this, so the weights of all residents in the home need to be ascertained and medical assistance should be obtained.

The PICU should secure records, assessments and get independent assessments of needs done for each resident in relation to staffing levels. If at this point the staffing levels are lower than the needs of the residents, a deliberate failure to act has occurred and the employer needs to be charged.

Falsification includes deletion or shredding of any records and also includes replacement of any original records.

Notes:

Who is not to be included in list of PICU independent advisors:

Anyone who has had employment or another role with the CQC or CSSIW unless they can be shown to be a genuine Whistle-blower under the Edna's Law criteria.

Anyone who has had a role in Safeguarding with the same provision as above.

Anyone who has had a role in the Freedom To Speak Up NHS Guardian scheme.

Anyone who has a past record of ignoring or harming Whistle-blowers or covering up wrongdoing.

Anyone who works for a government department in a policy-influencing or public relations role, for any of the above.

We are consulting on the suggested persons for expert input and a list of acceptable and ethical sources will be provided in part 2.

Summary

Part 3 of Edna's Law will consist of a comprehensive list of possible disclosures per industry compiled by the only experts acceptable to Compassion in Care i.e. Whistle-blowers.

These disclosures will include both situations which have already occurred and those which could arise. Attached to each disclosure will be the recommendations of how the investigation requirements should proceed for each industry. In short this will be a document that comprises a comprehensive list of potential disclosures and then what, how, when, where to ensure that PICU has all the relevant information.

We will call for the PICU to have the resources and knowledge to do the job and most importantly guarantee that there is full transparency throughout the process.

STEP FIVE Protection from victimisation and harassment.

This step is the only inter-movable step in the process because harassment and detriment can occur at any time and can take many forms. Edna's Law has no time limit on any future detriment that can occur to a Whistle-blower as a result of the whistle-blowing.

When can harassment and victimisation occur?
A Whistle-blower reports harassment internally and no action is taken.
A Whistle-blower reports concerns internally, and action is taken but then the Whistle-blower is targeted by their employer/accountable person due to the motive of resentment for being forced to take the action.
It should be noted that the Whistle-blower suffers the detriment for a lifetime.

Will Edna's Law protect against being bullied at work generally?
No, only if you are being bullied at work and a Whistle-blower reports this for you, then you become protected because the Whistle-blower stepped in to protect you.
There is no Me in whistle-blowing. If you are being bullied amongst a group of people and you report this, as long as the primary motive was to stop the bullying of all the group then that would qualify under whistle-blowing.
If you alone are being bullied or suffering harassment, then this is a serious work grievance, not whistle-blowing and we have to exclude it because the Edna's Law resources need to be directed at resolving public interest matters rather than individual work grievances.

What kind of harassment and detriment are Whistle-blowers subjected to?
How Edna's Law deals with this issue is very different to PIDA. PIDA's approach is like trying to catch smoke with a spoon and unfortunately PIDA currently protects against acts that are not harassment and are not victimisation.
Edna's Law recognises the devastating impact this has on the life of the Whistle-blower and how it is cumulative harm that builds over time and can impact mental and physical health long-term.
Extracts From Breaking the Silence see for full report
www.compassionincare.com

"I went to the manager and told her what I had seen. I thought that was the right way to do things. Now my life is hell and my shifts have all been changed, some of the staff

call me a grass.   The manager must have told them I had reported to her. I am afraid to go to anyone else."

"I was left to work on my own after speaking out about what was going on.   Many of the clients needed to be hoisted, I asked the company to help me, but they just said, "You are always complaining" People were crying to go to the toilet. It was dreadful, hour after hour. I kept going and asking the manager for help, but no-one would help me.   I was only trying to make it better for the clients when I blew the whistle, but I have made it worse. I had no choice but to try and hoist someone on my own. It's like they were waiting for me to do this, as soon as I went to get the hoist someone saw me and the next thing, I know the manager is behind me saying "You're suspended for doing that on your own".   I was even reported as a risk to the client. I could not go back and the union or no-one would help me. They said I had no chance as I was the problem yet until I blew the whistle, I was considered competent at my job. I said this is harassment but my union and everyone else said harassment is someone shouting at you and asked, "Has anyone shouted at you?". They had not, it was worse than that, they used the people I cared about to get to me".

"I reported it to the manager and thought that was the procedure, nothing was done about things at all. The only thing that changed was my life was made hell. I am too afraid to go outside".

"I worked there for over ten years and never had a problem with my work, after blowing the whistle everything changed, I was sacked for being constantly late for work, I could not believe it but when I asked to see my file all these notes had been made, warnings I was supposed to have been given. I said this is all lies, this is because I blew the whistle, the manager said no, no-one will believe you and she was right".

"I reported it to the management, but nothing has been done about it. The attitude towards me has been awful. I could not go to XXXX it would get even worse and I am too afraid".

"I lost my pension too. I will be paying for being a whistle-blower forever it seems".

"How do you get your trust back, your hope? Things will never be the same."

"It wears you down having no money, not being able to get a job, some of my family did not understand. "You should have kept your mouth shut and you would be alright now." What breaks my heart is they're right, that should not be but it's true, I would still have my job. No-one cares and it serves me right for caring"

"I feel afraid every minute I'm there, the people abusing the clients just laugh at me and they are safe after all, it is me who is afraid now".

"Silence does not sound so bad, and had I not suffered it day in day out … it was worse than being screamed at, I just left.   I tried to get help and advice but was told I did not have a chance."

"I could not take any more, my GP signed me off sick and I could not go back. It is only when you stop……that it all hits you.   I knew what had happened to me was wrong, that I should have put up more of a fight when the first four solicitors said they could not take my case. I just sat and cried for weeks."

"I loved my job and loved my residents and I know I did the right thing to try and protect them but, in the end, I was suspended for abusing, it destroyed me, and the company even tried to put me on the abusers' list. It took eight months before I was told I would not be put on the list, but it was too late by then, I had resigned. I could never turn a blind eye to abuse and would be too afraid to report it after this."

"I was reported to the NMC, I became the one doing wrong as soon as I blew the whistle on abuse, I was left in a dreadful position. The NMC said there was insufficient evidence against me but of course I knew that already but had to wait months for them to tell me that. The people *abusing the patients had no action taken against them at all."*

"The manager just looked at me and said, 'See what it feels like to be accused of abuse.' She tried to get me listed as an abuser and even though there was no evidence, it was the waiting. I will never get over the fact that a manager who covered up abuse was left in her job. When I blew the whistle, she just did everything in her power to make me look like the bad person. I just resigned. I could not ever go back; I could never put myself in that position again. Only abusers are wanted and not people who care. I still feel like crying all the time and worry about the clients I had to leave behind, no-one would help me, I did ring three solicitors but had no money."

"I was a good worker and never had any complaint until I raised concerns and suddenly everything, I did was wrong, and it was made clear to me that I would be the one reported for abuse next."

"Things were so bad I started to sell things just to have enough for food. I applied for dozens of jobs but as soon as you were asked why you left your last job, you could see the change of expression, the distrust…"

"I rang PCAW (Public Concern At Work) protect after I had blown the whistle, they told me to settle, I told them the abuse was being covered up but they told me to forget about that as I had done my bit and I should get on with my life. If I had taken their advice I would never have gone to the Ombudsman" Delyth Jenkins – Inquiry report by Public Service Ombudsman for Wales ref 1999-200600720 investigation into complaints against Carmarthenshire County Council which, due to the persistence of Delyth Jenkins, eventually exposed the whole county's safeguarding failures.

"'It's just bad luck you can't get a job' some people would say to me, 'it surely can't be because you reported abuse.' I would have thought the same before I blew the whistle, but I

knew as soon as I said I was a whistle-blower I was not wanted."

"It is dreadful, I hate going to work now, I know I have always been good at my job, the only thing that has changed is that I blew the whistle, but now everything I do is wrong."

"I could not afford the heating so sat wearing my coat indoors. The bills are piling up and I could not sleep for the worry."

Quotes from Beyond the Façade re harassment:

"I asked Ann Davidson to bring a chair while Linda helped me lift Molly up, the next thing I knew I was hit hard in the back and my whole body went forward with the force of the blow and my head went down onto Molly's chest. She was still holding the chair she had smashed into my back and was still screaming abuse, 'You fucking make me sick you lot'. It was not even the sound of the other residents in the room crying, it was little Molly who put her hand up to my face and said are you alright."

"I remember the first time I walked to the laundry, the staff from the other units were suddenly there. There was a terrible silence at first followed by a torrent of abuse. People I had worked with for years and who I thought I knew, they turned into total strangers who I no longer recognised at all, they became part of a violent mob whose rage knew no limits…."we are going to lose our jobs because of you and your tale-telling'."

"You are going to pay for this. Wait till it's dark, we are going to get you in the car park."

'Here comes the scum' were typical jeers we suffered from the mob and behind the mob were the sneering faces of Carol Jones and Carole Newton from BUPA".

"It was May 1999, the investigation continued and so did the harassment, every hour you were in the building you were so afraid that it was a physical sickness you felt in your gut. There was only one thing worse than the harassment suffered the day before and that was the day yet to come….

I did not know when the next chair would smash into me or if the threats of physical violence would be carried out."

"Linda was trying to feed a resident and they were both crying, the cleaners were stood behind shouting 'Scum is what you are". It all seemed to be happening in slow motion and as they shouted the abuse, I notice how their faces were twisted....tears ran down Linda's face. I kept saying over and over in my head, God help us."

Causing harm, for example harassment or detriment or bullying, loss of wages or any other harm is a **criminal** offence under Edna's Law. This can be prosecuted as a sole offence or in conjunction with the failure to act on whistle-blowing disclosures, which is a separate criminal offence. In short, these are the main two criminal acts in Edna's Law.

The Edna's Law statutory notice and leaflet pack (which will be published in Part 2) states that harming, harassing; bullying a Whistle-blower is a criminal offence. This acts as a deterrent to other staff who might participate in any of the above.

If you are a Whistle-blower being subjected to harm, please do the following:

Keep a diary of incidents in a hardback book (not a reporter's notepad).

Inform your employer in an email using the "Whistle-blower Harm" form which is contained in your pack.

This should be sent to your employer's designated email, then **your employer has one hour** in which to suspend any staff who may be involved in misbehaviour and **ten days** to investigate and take effective action to remedy this.

If the harm to the Whistle-blower continues and no action is taken contact the PICU and report this because it is a crime.

Minimum investigation requirements by PICU for the crime of harming a Whistle-blower:

The investigation must do the following:

Take a preliminary statement from the Whistle-blower, pending gathering the evidence outlined below.

Visit the relevant premises, secure the Whistle-blower's employment file, obtain all Human Resources (HR) information and all information in relation to this individual Whistle-blower's case.

Check all paperwork and establish if any entries have been made in relation to the Whistle-blower's performance after the whistle-blowing. This indicates that against the Whistle-blower as a direct result of the whistle-blowing.

Obtain a further statement from the Whistle-blower in relation to this paperwork as key points may occur that need to be checked on review with the Whistle-blower.

Interview and take statements from all suspects.

Interview and take statements from all potential witnesses.

At any stage of the harassment/detriment, a Whistle-blower may decide to apply for other positions. Should there be any difficulties at any point in the future then the Whistle-blower has the right to contact the PICU, and the PICU should also obtain from prospective employers the references given by the current employer, as well as all the evidence in relation to this. This pins down the element of blacklisting in all its forms. It is a criminal offence under Edna's Law to blacklist or give untruthful references for any Whistle-blower because this counts as harming a Whistle-blower and can be prosecuted separately as a sole offence. Edna's Law ensures the Whistle-blower is safe where they are in their current place of work and that they will be safe in any future place of work.

All of these measures ensure that the Whistle-blower has the best chance of protection at the point the protection is needed, whether it be in their current employment or in any future employment where harm could occur as a direct result of the whistle-blowing.

STEP SIX. The Whistle-blower's right to challenge PICU

These are the key points for this step and the full pack will be published in Part 2.

The purpose of this step is to ensure that the Whistle-blower and those the Whistle-blower tried to protect are not failed by those whose role it is to investigate, and that any decisions made are subject to an unprecedented level of scrutiny at every step. This ensures:

Public trust in the rule of law

Public trust in the administration of justice

That every case prosecuted under Edna's Law is based on the evidence, and **ALL** the evidence

That every case not prosecuted has considered all the evidence

That no evidence is suppressed as "prejudicial"

That no innocent person is wrongly penalised

That no guilty person escapes accountability - no matter how high their position is

and last but not least

That the voices of people like Edna are heard throughout the whole process.

Edna's Law is the only law that challenges the current system which allows injustice to thrive, that challenges the complacency that has infected the legal system, to ensure that justice and the law mean the same thing.

It is expected that certain groups of people and organisations will be outraged by Edna's Law **and that is exactly why we need Edna's Law so much**. Those with the loudest voice, with the most power, are those who are currently heard. Edna's Law turns this upside down, by giving those with no voice and no power an **equal** chance of legal protection and justice.

From Beyond the Façade page 280:

How did the law protect Edna?

Extract from Private Eye 4th March 2005 by Heather Mills:

"Former care staff who made serious allegations of neglect, potentially fatal doping and mistreatment at Isard House, a BUPA-run care home near Bromley in Kent, have at last learned what action police took in response to a dossier of evidence they submitted three years ago: it was all but ignored. No statement was taken from any witness, no member of staff from the home was interviewed and BUPA itself was never even approached over the allegations. In fact, police notes suggest that just a few hours after three bundles of documents, mainly complex medical records, were submitted officers had already decided that no crime had been confirmed.

This is alarming since on face value the medical sheets seem to show that a number of elderly residents were given potentially fatal doses of powerful drugs. One resident, EP (Edna), had on four occasions been given a dose of tranquilliser that was nine times the daily prescribed dose, 30mls, and six times higher than what is considered safe for an elderly person.

Eye readers may also recall the case of Audrey Ford, another Isard House resident who was taken to hospital suffering from the side effects of a powerful anti-psychotic which should only be given to those suffering severe mental illness, like schizophrenia. She never recovered and the coroner recorded an open verdict."

The medication sheets referred to above were salvaged from all the medication records whilst the abusers were trying to burn them at Isard House and were among only a handful salvaged by the BUPA 7 and taken out of the home. This shows why it is **so** important for the police to secure evidence at the first opportunity.

This also shows why the police need to examine properly all of the evidence available to them and why Edna's Law ensures there is scrutiny of any investigations. **Edna could have been saved, she was failed by the police and she was failed by the law**.

When a case is not referred to the CPS, based on grounds of a lack of evidence, it should **not** mean based on any of the following:

a lack of reading the available evidence

a lack of understanding the available evidence

a lack of resources

a lack of due diligence or

an attitude of complacency.

One small thing could have saved Edna, but that one small thing was not there, i.e. scrutiny of the evidence.

All that Edna's Law does is to ensure that the evidence is properly considered.

In order that the Whistle-blower is given the best chance of challenging any decision by police "to take no further action" the Whistle-blower is entitled to a copy of the police report in relation to each offence that was investigated. *Please note that any identifying information will have to be redacted to comply with the rule of law.

A full and detailed breakdown of the investigation must be documented:

Included in the body of the report, full transcripts of the suspects interviewed, and the statements taken.

Full transcripts of witnesses interviewed, and statements taken, again with any identifying information redacted.

Copies of all documentary evidence obtained and considered in the investigation must be included in the body of the report.

Copies of all advice obtained, included in the body of the report.

Copies of all forensic evidence or an explanation as to why no forensic input was requested.

A response to each of the above and why it is not considered sufficient to proceed to prosecution.

All of the above points ensure that justice is seen to be done, by ensuring from the earliest stage that the **administration** of justice is seen to be done also.

The Whistle-blower has the right to challenge. Part 2 will contain a detailed guidance document showing how this should be done.   This will include examples of any inconsistent conclusions on evidence, citing the evidence, the page and the paragraph.

Those Whistle-blowers who because of literacy, language barriers, visual impairment or other disability require assistance to prepare a response will be provided with that assistance, resourced from the money raised from fines for breaches of the statutory notice (see Step 1).

The police must then respond to the Whistle-blower's challenge and can either review the case or can maintain their original stance.

The police's role is to decide if there is a case to answer and the CPS role is to decide, on the basis of the evidence forwarded to them by the police, if there is a legal ground for a prosecution.

If the police decide to uphold their original decision, the Whistle-blower has the right to an independent assessment (see Step 7), or the police can refer to the CPS if they accept the Whistle-blower's challenge.

STEP SEVEN

Please note again that Edna's Law Part 2 will include the fully detailed procedure. The following points are a summary of what that procedure will entail.

At this stage I think it should be made clear who **would not** be eligible to carry out independent assessments:

Public Concern at Work (PCAW) Now called Protect PCAW Whistle-blowers UK (WBUK)

CQC, CIW, or any connected individuals

Anyone involved in Freedom to Speak Up (FTSU) Local Guardian roles in NHS

Anyone connected with Government departments

We are currently considering the options of who would be eligible, and these will be detailed in Part 2.

The Whistle-blowers who require assistance at this stage to present their reasons for reconsideration must be provided with that assistance.

The assessor can decide one of two things:

That the case should be referred to the CPS for consideration (go to Step 8)

or

that there is no case to answer as stated by the police.

Then at this point the following evidence must be compiled into one document called **The Challenge Evidence File which will consist of:**

The original police report as sent to the Whistle-blower, detailing the reasons for the police's decision (with identities redacted in the document)

The full Whistle-blower response to the above

The police reply to the Whistle-blower

The submissions to the independent assessor

The independent assessor's report

Please note that the Challenge Evidence File follows each Step of the case and is added to by the authorities who take the decisions at each Step.

All must be published on the PICU website at the termination of the whole Edna's Law process, at whichever Step that happens, to allow for transparency, ensuring high standards are maintained throughout the investigation stages, and as a resource for journalists and campaigners.

STEP EIGHT, The CPS

As for all the 13 Steps, this is the outline of what the procedure will be, and the full details will be in part 2.

This is an area that clearly needs the transparency that only Edna's Law has built in, which is something that has never been done before.   Edna's Law is about those who act in the public interest, and it shows how any case decisions are taken transparently also in the public interest.

Because there is no "Me" in Whistle-blowing, there can be no personal agendas in taking these cases to just conclusions.

All cases prosecuted under Edna's Law must be based on the following principles:

All the evidence available is examined

Must not be on any personal agendas

That justice is not something allocated by bean counters, budgets or resources

That no political agenda is involved

That incompetence, complacency and indifference play no part

That those who truly risk all to serve the public interest do not have to rely on those who use the term "public interest" perversely

That the rule of law is applied to all and all should be treated equally, or it is compromised completely.

If the CPS decide there is no case to prosecute, they must also publish a detailed report giving full reasons which must be sent to the Whistle-blower for any challenge to be made.

The CPS must include in their report a full account of the evidence examined, and an explanation of why it is insufficient for a prosecution.

For consistency, reference to similar cases on the PICU archive should be made to show where the same decision was taken on similar evidence.

This will build up a database open to the public to see that there is consistency in how this law is applied in particular circumstances.

For transparency, references to similar cases on the PICU archive where similar cases succeeded in a prosecution or conviction. This ensures that if there was a case where there had been a conviction this has to be considered so the CPS do not consider any case in isolation, therefore opening up the whole process to public scrutiny in the public interest and according to the essence of Edna's Law.

A breakdown of hours spent reading the evidence submitted by the police must be documented.

Minutes of case discussions have to be sent to the Whistle-blower and then it follows the Challenge Evidence File in the interest of transparency.

The CPS must reply to the Whistle-blower's challenge.

STEP NINE   The Whistle-blower's right to challenge the CPS

This Step gives the Whistle-blower the same rights and assistance as those detailed in Step 6.

STEP TEN The Whistle-blower's right to independent assessment of the CPS decision.

This Step gives the Whistle-blower the same rights and assistance as those detailed in Step 7.

STEP ELEVEN At trial

For the first time, the Whistle-blower will be appointed a suitable barrister to represent their rights and to ensure fair redress.

STEP TWELVE   All Edna's Law cases must be heard before a jury because a jury is the greatest safeguard, we have in the justice system.

STEP THIRTEEN   Legal redress

As for all Steps, this is the general outline and the full details will be published in Part 2.

Education: Costs from judge will include education and retraining.

Relocation:

Whistle-blowers living in rural areas and small communities may struggle to find employment for that reason and relocation costs must be awarded to those who need to move to find employment.

<u>Health:</u>
Any costs incurred by the Whistle-blower, including future costs of counselling, must also be covered.
<u>Employment search:</u>
Any costs relating to support needed to obtain new employment should also be included.
<u>Loss of trust:</u>
This is the main award given under Edna's Law and will be fully detailed in Part 2 but we are currently considering a percentage of salary to reflect the long term harm done. Where the employer has a shortfall in any assets to pay the damages, the remaining amounts will be paid by the State and the employer would be pursued at a future point to recoup the amount.
Criminal injuries would be paid to any individual that the Whistle-blower was trying to protect who had suffered harm.

The Prescribed Regulator under Edna's Law:
The Public Interest Crime Unit (PICU).

List of Protected Persons:
Employees
Volunteers
Zero hours contract staff
Subcontractors
Students aged 17+
"Bank" and agency staff
Staff working abroad for British companies and NGOs
Student nurses, doctors, dentists and all those workplaces where student status is applied.

Supplementary Powers:
Full details will be included in Part 2 however we are considering that the court should have the power to seize assets where there is a risk of the employer/accountable person absconding and where there are circumstances involving vulnerable people, this is to ensure they get a consistency of care and that their needs are met, for example if a care home closed.
In such circumstances, for a period of three weeks before moving people out of a home, "one to one" care should be provided to each resident by a specific staff member who

should stay with the person throughout the move and remain with the person for four weeks after the move. The cost of this must be covered by the employer/accountable person, as must any costs that have incurred in moving to the new home.

A recent case was where the owner of the home made huge profits from providing appalling care, and then escaped **any** accountability other than being struck off by the Nursing & Midwifery Council, which is not accountability for a millionaire who does not need to work. Those who had to move from the home were not given the required level of support but instead were moved at night with very little notice, no emotional support whatsoever and this will not be allowed to happen under Edna's Law. See www.compassionincare.com Merok Park

There are numerous situations where people have been adversely affected by the situation that led to the whistle-blowing and this needs to be considered also.

For example, those families who have lost loved ones at Southern Cross Orchard View care home have recently called for a public inquiry saying they were failed by the safeguarding review which is how many people feel after having to use a process that is fundamentally flawed.

Edna's Law will include victim impact statements at trial, and these must be considered when sentencing, to include the accountability that such families deserve.

Edna's Law Part 2 will include all details on penalties, prison terms, redress and other costs.

Chapter Ten.
Summary and Conclusions:

In this final section I would like to return to the question of independent assessors and why I have listed certain people who should not be included for this role. Compassion in Care not only recognises the heart of public interest but operates on those principles.

Compassion in Care is a registered charity which exposes abuse, raises awareness on whistle-blowing and has published comprehensive evidence in support of our work. We have helped, advised, supported thousands of families who have a relative in a care setting who has suffered abuse.

We have helped over 7000 Whistle-blowers, supporting them as best we can with the small resources we have, throughout the trauma, hardship and smearing that follows doing the right thing.

For those who fall into the 10% of Whistle-blowers who are able to access the law, we have done our best to provide a court companion and have helped assemble evidence and have transcribed proceedings. We have very limited resources but always do our best. It has at no time ever occurred to us to charge a fee. Compassion in Care has no paid staff, the helpline is run by me, initially with me working evenings as a cleaner so that I was able to run the helpline during the day. Over time the helpline has grown to such a degree that I did not have enough time to run the helpline and work elsewhere.

When I had to give up my night cleaning it was because I was able to claim a small amount towards my expenses. For the twelve hours I work each day I get in effect, 50p an hour allowing me to spend the time running Compassion in Care. For this reason, we survive. I ask readers to look at the work we have done:

Being a national charity that has in the words of a Department of Health official "changed things for the better", compare our work with any other similar organisation.

Compare our yearly budget with any other organisation. We operate on less than £10k per annum and we struggle every day on scant resources to help those in need.

The budget for "The Whistler" which we also run and is not a charity is zero - it is run on nothing more than Whistle-blowers caring about other Whistle-blowers.

There are other organisations that see whistle-blowing cases as an opportunity to make money out people at a time of vulnerability. See Complicit in Compliance chapter.

The impediment of PIDA

Having a whistle-blowing law that 90% of Whistle-blowers cannot access is contrary to the rule of law. Those 10% who do manage against all the odds to access PIDA are completely failed by a law that does not comply with the basic requirements and is therefore contrary to the rule of law.

Speaking to genuine Whistle-blowers every day, seeing the suffering and hardship that is the penalty of doing the right thing, then seeing the word "Whistle-blower" bestowed on people who lack the integrity and courage to walk in a genuine Whistle-blower's shoes for an hour angers me, but worse than this is that PIDA has protected the self-serving and manipulative, whilst failing the genuine - this is contrary to the rule of law.

I have cited the case of Patricia Douglas in my definition of public interest because I recognise in this case the elements that define the public interest for me: **that even in the most extreme of circumstances the human spirit can rise above self and express concern for others - that capacity is for me the essence and the spirit of the public interest and it is something that I can recognise in an instant.**

I am proud to know so many genuine Whistle-blowers. I am deeply ashamed of the country that I live in that allows such laws as PIDA to stand and I challenge every judge in England to read this book and do one of two things:

State they believe in the rule of law and therefore will actively support the introduction of Edna's Law

or

They can hang their heads in shame along with every successive Government that has failed to protect Whistle-blowers and has ignored evidence from Compassion in Care.

Final and important note to politicians:
Any theft of copyright from this book will result in a
prosecution for that theft of copyright.
This law is being put before the people for support, because
the alternative is to, put it through the House of Lords and
Commons and ask each individual who sits in both houses,
who has an interest in any company to excuse themselves
from this vote. Alas there would not be many left in the room,
which raises the question, what kind of democracy do we
have?
Eileen Chubb©
The end of injustice – the beginning of Edna's Law

All who read this please write to your MP and ask them to
support Edna's Law. Follow the link to the Edna's law
petition on the Compassion in Care Web-site

**At the time of going to print: As a result of the work we
have done to expose the self-serving agenda that is
exploiting whistle-blowers, WBUK are now under
investigation by The FCA for running an unlicensed
Case management Business,**

Printed in Great Britain
by Amazon

36107502R00098